BEYOND
comprehension

WHO IS GOD AND WHY IT MATTERS

C BOUWMAN

In deep gratitude for all that the L<small>ORD</small> God
has given to us over the years in the
Free Reformed Churches of Australia.
It is truly *beyond comprehension*.

Copyright © 2024

ISBN 978-1-7635447-3-4

Pro Ecclesia Publishers
Armadale, Western Australia
www.proecclesia.com.au

Design and layout: E Visser

contents

one — 9
The modern west and the identity of God

two — 17
What is God's love?

three — 29
God is simple – or complicated?

four — 40
God is holy – how AWESOME is that?!

five — 53
God is Almighty: What does Al mean?

six — 66
The Fear of God

Beyond Comprehension: who is God and why it matters

Of all the amazing things in this world, one of the most wonderful is surely this: eternal, almighty, infinite God has *told people-of-dust about himself*. That very fact means we would be remiss if we failed to listen carefully to his self-revelation.

In today's western civilization some people completely ignore God and his revelation on the assumption God does not exist. Other people twist what he has revealed about himself to justify a preferred understanding of who God is. Both stances produce a civilization where the *God*ness of God is scrubbed away from daily life – be it as a topic of conversation or as a source for responsible decisions.

That's the air that we and our children daily breathe. So it seems to me necessary that steps be taken to correct the unhealthy consequence of always inhaling polluted spiritual air. That is the intent of this brief publication.

I had the privilege of delivering this material in a series of post-confession classes in the Niagara Peninsula in the Fall of 2022. Early in 2023 my wife and I received the distinct privilege to return to the land where we'd raised our children - Australia - where I could again deliver this material in the Perth area in a series of lectures sponsored by *Seek Wisdom*, a study centre in the Free Reformed Churches of Australia. The second kick at the can gave me the opportunity to expand and improve the material with a view to eventual publication.

At the end of the series in Australia it became evident to me that a sixth paper was needed to tie the material together, namely, on the Fear of God.

It is my prayer that the material now presented for publication may be a blessing to many in Australia and Canada, and indeed around God's wonderful world. Soli Deo Gloria!

Clarence Bouwman,
Smithville, ON
August 2023

The modern west and the identity of God

The *Belgic Confession* (1561) has captured in accurate terms the historic position of the Christian Church on the question of *who God is*. Its opening article reads as follows:

> *We all believe with the heart and confess with the mouth that there is only one God, who is a simple and spiritual being; he is eternal, incomprehensible, invisible, immutable, infinite, almighty, perfectly wise, just, good, and the overflowing fountain of all good.*

With this formulation the confession's author, Guido deBrès, put to words the classic understanding embraced by the church in the preceding fifteen centuries. His confession was also foundational to the church's thinking on the topic during the centuries that followed.

The Battle for God

In today's western world multiple perceptions concerning God's identity jostle for acceptance. Without claiming to be complete, I list the following:[1]

---

1 The list is borrowed with appreciation from Norman L. Geisler & H. Wayne House, *The Battle for God*, 2001.

1. **Theism**: God is the eternal, almighty, Creator of all things who continues to uphold and govern daily all he has created, including (from time to time) doing miracles. This is the classic position of the Christian faith as reflected in the quote mentioned above from the *Belgic Confession*. This classic position is also held by Judaism and (largely) by Islam.

2. **Deism**: God is the almighty Creator of all things but instead of governing all details in his world God keeps himself at arms' length and lets the world run by itself. We might think of a clockmaker who has completed his clock, wound it up, and gone home while the clock runs by itself in his shop. A study done some 20 years ago[2] showed that American Christian youth overall functionally embraced Deism. To their thinking God is real but somewhat detached from daily life, yet always ready to help in time of need; hence the phrase, "God is there for me". Further, this study showed that these American youth are convinced that this God wants them to be happy and (in terms of obligation) to be nice to another. In practical terms, whatever might be considered offensive or intimidating about God has been stripped away to leave simply a God who is friendly and supportive. The authors of the above-mentioned study coined the phrase *Moral Therapeutic Deism* to describe this viewpoint.

3. **Pantheism**: the term joins two Greek words together to capture the thought that "all [is] God". God, then, is identified with the universe so that all things are divine. This is traditional Hinduism, a teaching that found its way into North America in the 1960 & 70s. It has found expression in North America particularly in New Age thinking and influenced much of the music of the 70s and 80s. This thinking today dovetails with environmentalism (Green Theology): since nature is divine, we need to care for it (or even: nature 'gods' are angry at humanity's abuse of nature, hence the catastrophic storms…).

---

2 Christian Smith & Melinda Lunquist Denton, *Soul Searching: The Religious and Spiritual Lives of American Teenagers*, 2005.

4. **Panentheism**: this term adds the Greek preposition "en" (= *in*) to the earlier term to express the thought that "God [is] in all". This is the new theological kid on the block, blending elements of Deism & Pantheism. It holds that mighty God is *in* this world ("all") somewhat like a soul is *in* the body – distinct but inseparable. As a soul grows with the body, so God is presented as growing with the universe. That growth means there is *change* in God, development, maturing. The catalyst for change in God is the things that happen in his world, particularly the decisions people make. God does not know all that people are going to decide and so needs to adjust his plans and preferences in response to human decisions. This view is appealing because the notion of *change* (think: evolution) is celebrated all around us – and now is extended also to God. It is appealing also because it pictures people as having a hand on the steering wheel of history in the sense that God adapts to (some of) our decisions.

5. **Finite Godism**: God is small, finite. He created this world but is not able to control all things in the world he formed. Rabbi Harold Kushner is perhaps one of the best-known exponents of this view of God as he expressed it in his 1981 book, *When Bad Things Happen to Good People*. God, Kushner says, would love to prevent evil from happening (for he's loving) but is not able to because he is too small to control all things in this world. The alternative would be that God is mighty to prevent evil, but too small in love to bother preventing evil.

6. **Polytheism**: this term combines two Greek words that means "many gods". The notion that many gods existed (and competed for allegiance) was characteristic of the heathen religions mentioned in the Bible; think of Egypt, Canaan, the Greeks, the Romans. Today Mormonism as well as occultism hold to a multiplicity of gods. A variation of this position expresses itself in Pluralism: all religions are nothing else than different expressions of the same divine Being and so all religions lead to the same God.

7. **Atheism**: this term combines two Greek words that mean "no God". It holds that deities do not exist except as figments of

human imagination. This was the position held by Karl Marx, a thinker who has had a profound influence on the secular humanism embraced by today's radical left. Religion (and hence the existence of a god) is nothing else than a tool used by the elite to keep the masses under their control.

Where are we?

The question that necessarily arises is this: which of these seven positions best describes the real-life thinking of the average Reformed, Christian person?[3]

The default answer is to point to our Confessions and say that we're Theists (ie, # 1 above): we hold that God is the almighty Creator of all things and that he continues to uphold and govern this world. We love the confession of Lord's Day 1 of the *Heidelberg Catechism*: "He preserves me in such a way that without the will of my heavenly Father not a hair can fall from my head," and Lord's Day 10: "leaf and blade, rain and drought, … indeed, all things, come to us not by chance but by his fatherly hand."

I suspect, though, that in our daily decision-making processes we're actually more of a blend of #2 (Deists) and #4 (Panentheists). It seems to me that often, when we make a decision, we picture God as at arms' length from us (and so we don't ask first of all what God wants of us or think that our circumstances have come upon us by God's doing), and yet we assume that God "is there for us" and that God wants us to be happy. Further, I detect in our thinking an implicit acknowledgement that there is development in God so that his goal posts change to accommodate our preferences. In our thinking we say: since God wants us to be happy, and our sense of being happy arises from satisfying our inner tastes, God must be OK with me listening to my deepest feelings. If there is a clash between

---

[3] As mentioned in the Introduction, these lectures were initially prepared for audiences in the Canadian Reformed Churches and the Free Reformed Churches of Australia. However, an assessment pertaining to the members of these churches would find outcomes similar to reformed Christians in other churches.

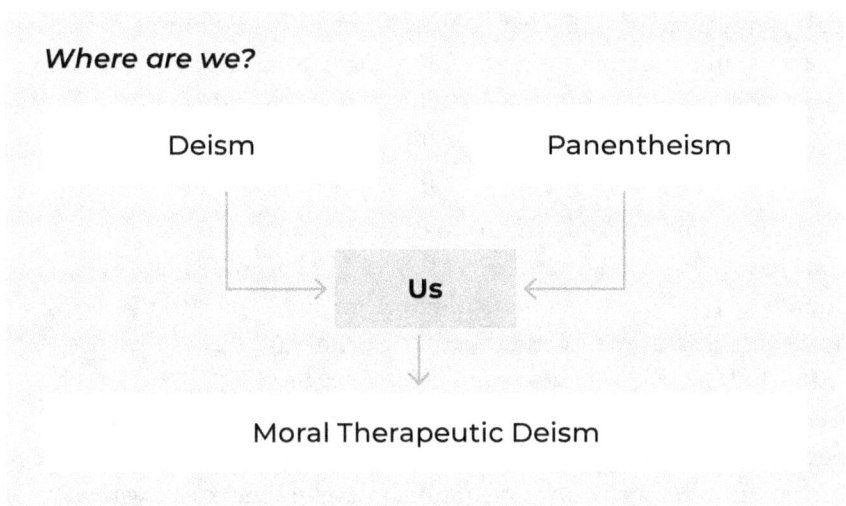

my feelings and the Bible, we end up massaging texts of Scripture so that they support our desires. In a word, Moral Therapeutic Deism has a much stronger hold on us than we commonly acknowledge. And no, I do not think this blend typifies only the younger amongst us.

I need a couple of examples to give colour to this assessment. In time past, divorce was heavily frowned upon within the churches and remarriage after divorce even more so. That was because the Word of God is so clear about God's thoughts and instruction in relation to this topic.[4] A nod to #1 -God is the almighty Creator and so in a position to write an authoritative Operators' Manual for how to do life well in the difficult circumstances he permits- means that in an unhappy marriage we ask: what does the Lord want of me (eg, do I need to repent of sinful conduct, how do I best keep my vow "till death us do part"), and so we refuse to consider divorce as a viable backdoor escape from an unhappy marriage. More, when you end up single you again ask: what does the Lord want of me (eg, is this the cross that comes with following Christ). But a nod to #2 means that

---

4   See, for example, the historic *Form for the Solemnization of Marriage,* available at www.canrc.org/forms/form-for-the-solemnization-of-marriage.

I ask: with God at somewhat of a distance, what route must I choose to escape my unhappiness and achieve a greater degree of happiness, and a nod to #4 means that I accept that with changing culture God's goal posts can change too. The result: what was unacceptable in our churches a few decades ago is acceptable today.

A second example relates to commitment to church. In time past it was largely understood that God has joined us to his church (yes, locally) so that we might serve and be served by one another (think of the instruction of 1 Corinthians 12). In keeping with #1 above, the rule was: even if the preacher God gives doesn't have a captivating style, or even if the fellow members God has put on my path are not 'my type', we leaned into maximizing our contribution to positive congregational development. But with a nod to #2, the decisive criteria becomes: am I happy in this church? So: does this church fulfil my needs? Add a dose of #4 and we end up with patterns of doing church far removed from what the fathers understood God required of them in his Word.

I could also mention current developments relating to gender. Some in our midst leave themselves open to the persistent message of our culture: you must listen to your inner voice to be happy – and happiness is your right. Your inner voice has something divine in it (recall #4 re Panentheism) and that's especially true in relation to sexuality. So while the older in our midst shake their heads at the perceived absurdity of gender being fluid, the younger see (or want) space for public expression and acknowledgement of your inner identity. Others ought not to criticize your expression of your inner self because God wants you happy and he changes in step with human development.

Fruit

This tacit embrace of Moral Therapeutic Deism in our real-life decision-making processes explains (in part) other phenomena that have risen in prominence in our midst in the last number of years. Two examples come to mind.

There is among the members of the churches an increase in the level of anxiety. Elders are more busy dealing with stress and/or its fallout than they were in the past. Similarly, there is more need for (professional) counselling today than there used to be. And to be clear: I'm grateful that elders are engaging the stressed in our midst and that congregants are seeking professional help when needed. Yet I fear that the reason for this increased anxiety is that in our thinking God is at arms' length from our real lives, and that though he wants us happy we're not finding lasting happiness by satisfying our feelings. So Biblical expressions as "God is my Rock and my Fortress" don't resonate the way they ought, and a sense of peace and safety seems more elusive. And words as those of the *Heidelberg Catechism* in Lord's Day 9 -"In him I trust so completely as to have no doubt that he will provide me with all things necessary for body and soul"- come across as surreal.

A second example relates to restlessness in relation to how we do life and hence an urge to change things up from the traditions of the past. Please note: I will not make the case that the way the fathers did things was just right. But the three examples I mentioned above all speak to an inner restlessness – and such impatience does not make for stability and so for space to work on what's actually important, ie, walking humbly and dependently with the Lord in all life's challenges. It all serves as a *distraction*.

How to counter this?

I'm reminded of a statement Martin Luther voiced in relation to Erasmus: "Your thoughts of God are too small." So is the God of #2 (Deism) and #4 (Panentheism) as listed above. Luther himself, of course, embraced #1, classical Theism, because that's the God of Biblical revelation. That's the position we need to recapture. That involves turning away from a shrunken perception of who God is and embracing his revelation about himself as a God of infinite majesty.

In this regard there is wonderful assistance from the writings of numerous Neo-Calvinists. In distinction from more Arminian-minded preachers as Billy Graham (promoting a smaller God who waits patiently for people to open their hearts to him), James Packer published *Knowing God* in 1973 and RC Sproul published *The Holiness of God* in 1985. Both books contributed greatly to my appreciation for the Godness of God as confessed in Article 1 of the Belgic Confession. In their wake are numerous preachers and writers across North America today who boldly draw out the greatness of God and its blessed consequences for the life of the Christian. Names as John Piper, Al Moehler, John McArthur and Alistair Begg come to mind.

In subsequent articles I plan to reconstruct in our hearts and minds what it is we actually confess about God in the *Belgic Confession*. A sound understanding of the identity of God is absolutely imperative because -as the old adage has it- getting doctrine right is the first step to getting life right.

What is God's love?

In the previous chapter I shared my concern that in our decision-making processes Reformed people are frequently not acting in step with what we confess in Article 1 of the *Belgic Confession* (quoted below). Instead, in our decision-making processes we often imagine God to be removed some distance from us so that we don't see our circumstances as coming from his sovereign and Fatherly hand, and we imagine God wishing us happy and being largely OK with what we decide. This tacit embrace of Moral Therapeutic Deism results in an increased level of anxiety as well as impatience with how the fathers used to do things.

My intent in the present chapter is to draw out that (mentally) placing God some distance from us (so as to gain some greater freedom in making our decisions) in fact *impoverishes* us. Every circumstance the Lord God sovereignly puts on our path and every command he gives us in untangling the pressures of the circumstance has been and continues to be a display of this *love*. Appreciating the *love of God* is the antidote we need to Moral Therapeutic Deism.

Love in the Belgic Confession

Today's western culture celebrates "love". Yet when Guido deBrès penned Article 1 of his *Belgic Confession*, he included among the attributes of God no reference to "love". He wrote:

> *We all believe with the heart and confess with the mouth that there is only one God, who is a simple and spiritual being; he is eternal, incomprehensible, invisible, immutable, infinite, almighty, perfectly wise, just, good, and the overflowing fountain of all good.*

I won't speculate why deBrès did not mention "love" (or similar Biblical words as "mercy", "kindness", "grace") in his list. Certainly for us today, as we make it our business to come to grips with *who God is*, we'd be remiss to bypass God's love. I say that for a number of reasons:

- "Love" is such a buzzword in today's western culture.
- To the degree God is acknowledged in our culture, he's pictured as stern and grumpy and wagging a warning finger at sinners instead of being loving and having open arms to welcome prodigals. The attributes of God listed in Article 1 tend more to reinforce than to correct that perception.
- Scripture itself says, "God is love" (1 John 4:8,16).

DeBrès himself, we need to know, was keenly aware that his list of divine attributes in Article 1 was not complete. He writes in Article 16, for example, that "God manifested himself to be *as he is*" – and explains: "merciful and just". The word "just" appears in Article 1, but "merciful" does not. In fact, as we read through the whole *Belgic Confession*, it's striking how often -and how centrally- deBrès refers to God's love and mercy and grace and other similar descriptive words of God. Consider the following (incomplete) selection:

- Article 8 concerning the Trinity: "they are all three one, in truth, in power, in goodness, and in mercy."
- Article 12 concerning the angels: "some of these have fallen…, but the others have by the grace of God remained steadfast…"
- Article 13 concerning God's providence: "nothing can happen to us by chance, but only by the direction of our gracious heavenly Father."
- Article 15 concerning sin: "original sin is not imputed to the children of God … but by his grace and mercy is forgiven them."
- Article 17 concerning God's response to our fall: "our gracious God in his marvellous wisdom and goodness set out to seek man when he trembling fled from him."

- Article 20: "We believe that God, who is perfectly merciful and just, sent his Son ... to bear the punishment of sin... God ... poured out his goodness and mercy on us... Out of a most perfect love he gave his Son to die for us..."
- Article 26 concerning Christ's intercession: "could we find one who loves us more...?"
- Article 33 concerning sacraments: "We believe that our gracious God ... has ordained sacraments ... to be pledges of his good will and grace towards us."
- Article 36 concerning government: "We believe that ... our gracious God has ordained kings, princes, and civil officers."
- Article 37 concerning Paradise Restored: "As a gracious reward, the Lord will grant them to possess glory such as the heart of man could never conceive."

From this list it is clear that deBrès not only knows of God's love (and similar terms) but readily confesses its central role in God's identity and hence activity. I would think it accurate to suggest that to deBrès' thinking God's love and mercy and kindness, etc, are not so much attributes that belong alongside those listed in Article 1 as attributes that *overarch* those of Article 1. To say it differently, God's love is the lens through which we need to examine his other attributes.

Challenges

As mentioned, the concept of love is highly celebrated in our present culture. We hear in the term overtones of being nice, being tolerant, giving the other space to be themselves in non-judgemental fashion. If we were to import that loading of the term love in relation to God, we'd have to describe him as soft on sin. We'd also invariably end up describing his justice as today's culture does, ie, standing up for the disadvantaged at the expense of the oppressive elite. So we need to watch out that we load the term love *Biblically* as opposed to (might I say) *westernly*.

A second challenge facing us is that the term "love" is a slippery word, one hard to grasp. To illustrate, consider its texture in the following two sentences:

- I love my wife.
- I love ice-cream.

We consider it self-evident that my love for my wife has a different quality and content than my love for ice-cream (and vice versa). But to describe the difference is not so easy to do. In the Bible, as it turns out, the word "love" also has multiple textures in relation to God. The challenge is to notice these different loadings of the word and understand their significance.

Textures

As we seek to get a handle on the love of God, we need to do more than look at passages that literally use the word "love". I say that because (as indicated above) the Biblical concept of God's love comes to us through multiple words, including "mercy", "grace", "kindness", etc. Each such word certainly has its own nuance, yet each contributes to God's revelation concerning his love. Further, there are passages in Scripture that describe God's love (and mercy and kindness, etc) without mentioning the word. We need to work with the entire revelation of Scripture as we seek to grasp the multiple textures of God's love. Consider, then, the following nuances:[5]

1. There is love within the Trinity, specifically from the Father to the Son, cf John 3:35; 5:20; 17:24. This love was there before the Creation of the world and so is an out-of-this-world 'sort' of love that's beyond creature's ability to fully grasp.

2. There is a kindness and tender care in God towards the world he created. After he finished creating, God did not desert his handiwork but continued to uphold and govern it directly. That's true also after the fall into sin, as Jesus said (as illustration of what love looks like), "he makes his sun rise on the evil and on the good, and sends rain on the just and on the unjust" (Mt 5:45).

3. God has a saving stance toward his fallen creation, cf John 3:16: "God so loved the world that he gave his only Son."

---

[5] With thanks to Don Carson, *The Difficult Doctrine of the Love of God*, pg 16ff.

4. God loves particular persons in distinction from others so as to elect them to salvation, cf Dt 7:7f; Eph 1:3ff.
5. Jesus told his disciples to "abide in my love" by keeping his commandments, John 15:9f; cf Jude 21. This implies the possibility of falling out of God's love so that in some way God's love is conditional.

What is God's love?

1.	**Intra-Trinitarian**	John 17:24; 3:35; 5:20
2.	**Providential care of Creation**	Matt 5:44f; Rom 2:4
3.	**Saving stance to fallen world**	John 3:16; Ex 34:6f
4.	**Elect to salvation**	Deut 7:7f; Eph 1:3ff
5.	**Conditional love**	Jude 21; John 15:9f

It's self-evident that the nuances of the term "love" are far from identical in these five points[6]. The love within the Trinity (#1) involves no forgiveness or redemption, unlike God's love to his fallen world (#3) or to the elect (#4). God's love for his elect (#4) is not a carbon-copy of the love that prompted him to send his Son into the world (#3), for the unbelieving inhabitants of the world will experience God's eternal wrath while its believing inhabitants will experience eternal glory.

These differences in nuance also help us in the proper use of some common clichés. Can we say to anyone, "God loves you"? The answer is Yes if the word "love" is understood in terms of #2 or #3 above, but No if it's understood in terms of #4. Again, can we say, "God loves you unconditionally"? Yes, if with the word "love" you

---

6 This list is clearly not complete but simply representative of possible textures.

mean #2,3 or 4, but No if you mean #5. In other words, it all depends on what you mean with the word "love".

God is love

Given this elusiveness in how the Bible uses the term "love", is an attempt to grasp its bottom meaning futile? John writes that "God is love" (1 John 4:8,16) – but are we left to guess which of the possible nuances listed above this might refer to? Thankfully, God's care and mercy and kindness to us is so great that he has not left us in the dark as to what his identity as "love" actually means. In an effort to gain greater clarity, let's work our way once more through the five textures of God's love as listed above, this time slower and with greater detail.

Trinity

The love of God within the eternal Persons of the Trinity is foundational inasmuch as this love precedes every expression of God's love within his creation. He has not told us much about the love between the three Persons[7], but has revealed enough for us to grasp its fundamental flavour. Jesus hints at that flavour in his high priestly prayer, "Father, I desire that they also, whom you have given me, may … see my glory that you have given me because you loved me before the foundation of the world" (John 17:24). Jesus says here that the Father has *given Jesus glory* and done so *because he loves him*. The point is: the Father's love is *enriching toward the Son*.

We can fill in some further detail on this glory through other words Jesus spoke. For example, "the Father loves the Son and has given all things into his hand" (John 3:35). The word "and" in that sentence connects the two parts of the sentence so as convey that the Father's love for the Son receives expression by his having "given all things into his hand". A couple of verses earlier Jesus had indicated that this "giving" occurred before he came to earth (as 17:24 also says). The gift God gave, "all things", describes the world itself. The

---

7   We read only of the Father's love to the Son, not of his love to the Holy Spirit or the Spirit's love to the Father and the Son. We need deliberately to avoid speculation as we seek to use our creaturely imagination to fill the gaps.

well-being of God's whole creation was entrusted to the Son. How he executes his task will determine his glory.

More detail arises from another word Jesus spoke. "Truly, truly, I say to you, the Son can do nothing of his own accord, but only what he sees the Father doing. For whatever the Father does, that the Son does likewise. For the Father loves the Son and shows him all that he himself is doing" (John 5:19f). We're to realize that Jesus spoke these words in an economic and social reality wherein a son took over the trade of his father. It fell to the father, then, to teach his son the tricks of the trade and for the son to do whatever the father was doing. Clearly, the greater the love between father and son, the more precise the "showing" and the more careful the following. Now Jesus speaks of the Father's love for the Son being such that the Father "shows him all that he himself is doing" – teaching him (might I say) the tricks of the trade. And such is the love of the Son for the Father that "whatever the Father does, that the Son does likewise" – learning and doing the tricks of the trade. Going to the cross to atone for sin was not something the Son thought up himself but was a work the Father "showed" the Son. Through fulfilling the Father's instructions the Son would receive glory, ie, he would bask in the Father's eternal approval of his work.

These few hints show us that the love of the Father for the Son is not selfish, ie, Father/self-centred, but his Son/other-centred. More, the point of this love is the *enrichment* of the other. (Of course, this goes two ways, cf 1 Cor 15:28.)

Providential care

God's creation daily benefits from his continued care. Adam and Eve in Paradise, as well as all plants and animals in the Garden, flourished under God's affection for his world. They didn't simply survive; they *thrived* in a context of happiness and pleasure as God habitually came to walk and talk with his creatures, cf Gen 3:8. Though after the fall into sin this world has become a wilderness (Gen 3:17ff), God stills seeks to *enrich* his creatures through the benefits of sun and rain (Mt 5:45) and ultimately the gift of his only Son (John 3:16). Through his grace and kindness sinners suffering from "thorns and thistles" (Gen 3:18) should come to experience "fullness of joy" (Ps 16:11). God's love is the *enrichment* of the other.

Forgiveness

This depth of what is meant by the love of God comes out gloriously in Ex 34:6f: God passed in front of Moses on Mt Sinai and proclaimed,

> *"The L*ORD*, the L*ORD*, a God merciful and gracious, slow to anger, and abounding in steadfast love and faithfulness, keeping steadfast love for thousands, forgiving iniquity and transgression and sin, but who will by no means clear the guilty, visiting the iniquity of the fathers on the children and the children's children, to the third and the fourth generation."*

Notice first the number of synonyms the Lord uses here, all catching aspects of his love: mercy, grace, slow to anger, steadfast love, faithfulness, forgiving. (A passage as this illustrates why it's insufficient to simply do a word study on "love" as we seek to grasp what God's love is.)

The context in which the Lord uttered these words of self-revelation are enlightening. Consider the following:

1. The fall into sin is a present and harsh reality, with every person on Planet Earth a rebel deserving of God's eternal judgment.

2. Moses (and Israel with him) was deeply aware of how low-down and destitute and hopeless Israel was in their enslavement to Pharaoh. There was simply nothing attractive about this dead-beat nation of slaves.

3. At Mt Sinai the Lord officially established a bond of love with these ex-slaves, with the famous words, "I am the LORD your God, who brought you out of the land of Egypt, out of the house of slavery" (Ex 20:2). Ex-slaves were now *his* people, he now *their* God. In recognition of such grace, Israel must never generate an image of God in any fashion (Ex 20:4ff). But here they were, a short six weeks after God officially tied the knot with this people and forbade an image – dancing around a golden calf meant to depict God (Ex 32). Here was every reason

for the Lord to kick lousy Israel to the gutter and destroy them as he had the Egyptians through the plagues and the sea – a possibility Moses and Israel had themselves recently witnessed.

That's the setting in which the Lord uttered the words of Ex 34:6f. That context takes our breath away; why, O why, would the Lord be "merciful and gracious, slow to anger, and abounding in steadfast love" to a low-down people who just spurned his love in deliberate disobedience?! The answer to that question, of course, is the element I didn't yet mention, viz, he had already given Moses instruction on how to build the tabernacle (Ex 25-31) – where God would dwell in the midst of these ex-slaves in the Most Holy Place. The people ought to die because of their sins, but the lamb sacrificed on an altar located strategically between God and his people spelled out that another would die in their place – Jesus Christ in the fullness of time. *They* would be spared because *he* would be condemned. *They* were adopted because *he* would be rejected. *They* would be enriched because *he* would lay all his glory aside.

Glory!

What *is* God's love? At its heart is the word *enrichment*. Paul puts it like this: "And we all" -sinners each!- "beholding the glory of the Lord, are being transformed into the same image from one degree of glory to another" (2 Cor 4:18). Christ had prayed that God's elect might "see my glory that you have given me because you loved me" (John 17:24). Paul confirms that we see it -present tense!- in this life already *and are ourselves being changed to image that glory*. That's sanctification today and it's glorification tomorrow! Today this life is still a veil of tears, but when Christ returns we'll experience "an eternal weight of glory beyond all comparison" (2 Cor 4:17). As deBrès put it in Article 37: "as a gracious reward, the Lord will grant them to possess glory such as the heart of man could never conceive." In the New Jerusalem we creatures will finally grasp (though not fully) the infinite depths of God's out-of-this-world love – an endless depth flowing out of the heart of his own being.

And notice the word "possess" in the last quote. Glory is *God's*, yet Christians may "possess" it. The point is that the Lord would *share* his glory with people, with finite creatures, sinners, *prodigals*. Such is the extent of his *enrichment!*

Holy love

There is nothing on Earth like God's love. It's not sentimental nor rooted in God's (changing?) feelings. It's not selfish as if the Lord is giving only to get. It's not impoverishing as if the Lord becomes vulnerable or weak on account of serving the other. It is *enriching* for the undeserving in this sense that God would have creatures -sinners at that- *bask in his glory*, share what's glorious about God. It is *endless* because infinite God himself *is* love. This is an out-of-this-world love, a *holy* love – utterly unique from anything you find in this life.

This is the love of God deBrès was happy to confess. Consider the following quotes again:

1. Article 15 concerning sin: "original sin is not imputed to the children of God … but by his grace and mercy is forgiven them."
2. Article 17 concerning God's response to our fall: "our gracious God in his marvellous wisdom and goodness set out to seek man when he trembling fled from him."
3. Article 20: "We believe that God, who is perfectly merciful and just, sent his Son … to bear the punishment of sin… God … poured out his goodness and mercy on us… Out of a most perfect love he gave his Son to die for us…"
4. Article 26 concerning Christ's intercession: "could we find one who loves us more…?"
5. Article 37 concerning Paradise Restored: "As a gracious reward, the Lord will grant them to possess glory such as the heart of man could never conceive."

This is not a divine attribute that should have a place beside the others listed in Article 1; this is the *overarching* attribute, the one that exposes the very heart of God to us. This identity of God gives the lie to a depiction of God as stern, grumpy, wagging an unhappy index finger at us. This identity of God draws a picture of open arms for every prodigal, no matter how destitute (see Luke 15:11ff). Only with such a God can a sinner dare cry out for mercy and be confident of the Lord's answer. He *is* love!

Implications

1. Everyone honest person is aware of his/her own sinfulness. Moods that don't comport with basking in God's mercy settle so comfortably upon us, thoughts that blaspheme God arise unwittingly in our minds, desires that wish harm upon a neighbour appear out of the blue, words that hurt fall unbeckoned out of our mouths, and deeds that promise to satisfy our sense of well-being away from God come so irresistibly upon us… Then: what picture of God arises in our minds? A warning finger or welcoming arms? A stern look that tells us to clean up our mess before we come to him? Or a face of compassion because Christ already took the judgment we earn? Remember G.R.A.C.E.: God's Riches At Christ' Expense. It's tasting his welcoming arms, basking in the holy love we've spurned, that drives to heartfelt repentance.

2. God's love is not simply being tolerant or nice to people. That's far too passive a presentation of God's love. He has the well-being of undeserving people in mind and so in love, mercy, kindness directs sinners to Jesus Christ as the only way to happiness – eternally so. Even the unpleasant events that he sovereignly puts on our path are wrapped in this love – though at the moment it does not appear to us to be so, cf Heb 12:10.

3. As we parent our children or perhaps visit among the brotherhood, we need to be deliberate in generating an understanding of God that agrees with who he is: "God is love". Those we teach and lead and encourage need to see in the eye of their mind the welcoming arms of triune God who would enrich sinners, those undeserving of his grace. This presentation of God is the necessary corrective to the Moral Therapeutic Deism I mentioned previously. So great is his love

that he is always near, always seeking to *enrich* his children till we enter his presence in the full richness of eternal glory.

4. This is the texture of love God's people are to illustrate to the neighbour. As we seek to image God in marriage, parenting, at work, etc, our love is never to come with a selfish spin, but always simply to enrich the other – not matter how unworthy. The concept drives our conduct.

God is simple – or complicated?

Reformed Christians officially have big thoughts of God. Anyone reading the first article of the *Belgic Confession* could come to no other conclusion:

> *We all believe with the heart and confess with the mouth that there is only one God, who is a simple and spiritual being; he is eternal, incomprehensible, invisible, immutable, infinite, almighty, perfectly wise, just, good, and the overflowing fountain of all good.*

I suggested in the first contribution of this booklet that in our thinking we tend to a blend of deism and panentheism. That is: in our decision making processes we place God at arm's length from us with the understanding that he's there to help us (Moral Therapeutic Deism) when we need him; more, he wants us to be happy and so is open to bending his rules as he adapts to changes in our cultures. As antidote to Moral Therapeutic Deism I drew out in the previous contribution what God's *love* means. I argued that imagining the Lord God as somewhat removed from us (so as to give us liberty to make decisions on our own) is actually a tragic impoverishment; his love means that he *enriches* us, in this life and the life to come. No one in their right mind would wish a God of such love to be removed some distance from us; on the contrary.

In the present contribution I want to suggest an antidote to the panentheist streak I see in our thought processes, ie, the perception that God changes in step with human development and/or the influence we exert on him. The first descriptive term concerning God as mentioned in Article 1 helps us in this endeavour, namely, the word "simple".

What are we talking about?

The term "simple" confuses us. The common use of that word suggests that we're confessing here that God is dim-witted, naïve – which we know to be patently untrue. In fact, in its place we would expect to find here a term confessing how *complex* or *complicated* God is. For we earthlings struggle to get our heads around God's identity; he's beyond us, anything-but-simple.

A good dictionary will inform us that the word "simple" stands in contrast not only to the word "complicated" but also over against the term "compound". We learned in grade school that there are *compound words* in our English vocabulary, words made up of two (or more) other words, eg, pan-cake, sea-shore, water-slide. By contrast, non-compound words are "simple", meaning that they are made up of simply one part, eg, pan, cake, water. It's this latter use of the term "simple" that the *Belgic Confession* intends when it confesses that God is "simple", viz, he is not made up of multiple parts.

We come across compound entities wherever we look in our created world. A car is made up of wheels, doors, engine, transmission, wipers, and so many more parts. A person has arms, eyes, feet, a liver, etc. We would never say that the engine *is* the car, or the liver *is* the person; at best we would say that a car *has* an engine and a person *has* a liver. The part is never the whole. That's characteristic of this created world: *this* is never *that*. We differentiate.

That's true also when we dig to a deeper level. There are things in God's world that simply *exist* (a rock). There are other things that *exist and live* (a flower). There are also things that *exist and live and move* (a rabbit). And there are things that *exist and live and move and think* (people). Any of the above creatures are susceptible to *change*. A rock can roll from here to there – a change in location. A flower

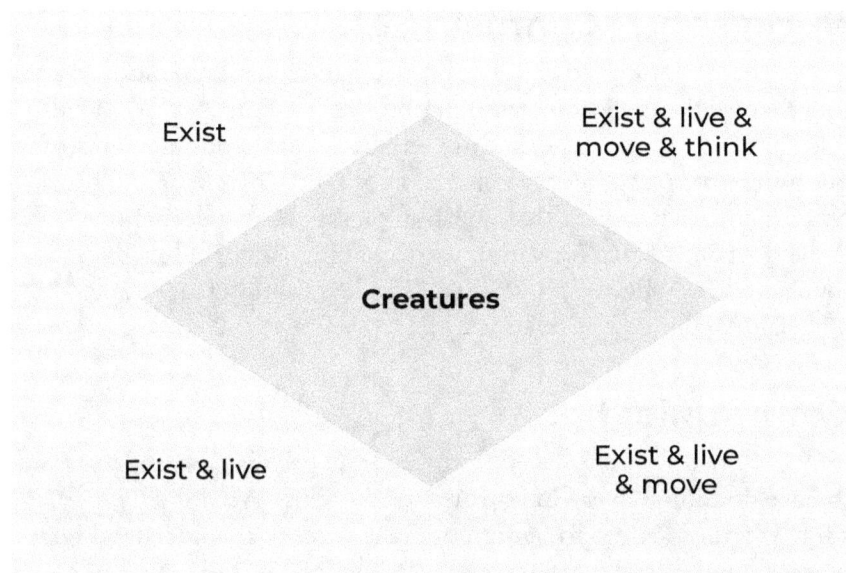

can bud, bloom and die – a change in its development. Because of compound statuses, life can be complex, with no two moments necessarily being unchangingly the same for any given creature.

Now the question is: must we say the same in relation to God? Are there *parts* to God, ie, arms and eyes and liver as we have? Does he have qualities (or attributes or parts or aspects or characteristics[8]) that belong beside each other (like parts of a car) that, when properly assembled, make up God? Article 1 mentions aspects as eternal, invisible, immutable, infinite, just, good. Is God, then, the sum of these parts properly assembled? And: is there *progress, growth, change, development* in God as there is in a rock (movement, erosion) or a flower (from bud to bloom) or a person (aging, learning, forgetting)? These are the sort of questions addressed in the word "simple". With this single word we confess that God is *not compound*, is not made up of parts. And so there is with God no change either.

---

8   It's hard to find the correct word to use here. Theologians are undecided and so I'll interchange the terms.

Necessary? Confusing?

The Scriptures attribute multiple characteristics to God. We're told that God *has* wisdom, truth, faithfulness, infinity, etc. We're also told that God *is* wise, true, faithful, infinite. Do these statements of Scripture not contradict the confession of God's *simplicity* and insist on his being *compound*? That question presses us to a deeper one: is the doctrine of *simplicity* even worth talking about? How does it touch are lives? Better: why would God reveal himself as simple – especially in our complicated world??

Communication

Humanity has received from God the privileged mandate to have dominion over God's world, Gen 1:26ff. Accordingly, we study whatever comes to our attention as we seek to understand how that item in God's creation works. The process of study involves examining *parts* and how the parts work together. Our (now fallen) inquisitiveness means we attempt to do the same with God. Metaphorically speaking, we try to put him on our table for dissection and examination, then we seek to reassemble his parts to discover how the parts make the whole, and ultimately write a book on God.

The difficulty is that we earthlings cannot climb into heaven to look upon, let alone examine, our Creator. Any attempt to do so necessarily ends up with nothing other than human speculation. It is possible to say an intelligent -let alone accurate- word about God only after the Lord has first revealed that word to us. A further difficulty is that we creatures, finite as we are, cannot understand divine, heavenly, communication; ours is a different "language" than is "spoken" in heaven. Communication (or revelation) from God must of necessity be in our "language", that is, almighty God must come down to our creaturely level if we are to understand anything he says.

In his goodness the Lord God is pleased to do so and speak to us in the *form* of a *man*. I italicize those two words because those two words provide the meaning of the essential theological word we now need: *anthropomorphic* (that's Greek: anthropos = man; morph = form). We are familiar with the concept from how a mother speaks to her baby; she gets down to her baby's level and babbles in baby-talk. That comparison catches what God does with us; he brings himself down to our level, to *man-form*.

How so? Our created world is necessarily made up of *parts*. God created time, so in our world *now* is never *then*; *today* is never *yesterday*. God created space, so in our world *here* is never *there*. Similarly, *this* (book) is never *that* (book, or post or plant). God himself is above time and space, ie, not restricted by *here* and *there*, *now* and *then*, *this* and *that*. As God speaks to us, he does so in our human categories. So he says that underneath Israel is his everlasting "arms" (Dt 33:27), and that his "eyes" travel the length and breadth of the globe (2 Chron 16:9). Yet we are not to conclude from such verses that God has physical parts as arms and eyes, as we have (cf John 4:24: "God is spirit"). God's reference to arms and eyes is an example of *anthropomorphism*, ie, of God coming down to our level and communicating in categories we can understand (including reassuring us of the comfort of his unending care and of nothing escaping his attention).

In a similar way, the Lord speaks of his goodness and wisdom and love and holiness, etc, and says too that he is life (John 1:5), is love (1 John 4:8), etc. We automatically set these qualities *beside* one another as so many different characteristics. But the Lord would have us know that his mentioning these qualities separately does not mean that God is therefore the sum-total of these qualities. He's speaking at our level. Since God himself is above time and space *here* can be *there* for him (he's omnipresent) and *before* can be *after*, *yesterday* can be *today*, and *this* can be *that*. His qualities, then, are all one and the same, ie, he *is* goodness and wisdom and power and existence, etc, all in one bundle. As the noted Dutch theologian Herman Bavinck put it, God "is the perfect and infinite fullness of being, an 'unbounded ocean of being'".[9]

Scripture

None of this is meant to sound philosophical or excessively heady – though I grant that it does. So I want to take a moment to

---

9   *Reformed Dogmatics*, II, 176.

show that this is simply what Scripture says.[10] Moses at the burning bush asked God what *name* he was to share with the enslaved Israelites to substantiate his calling to deliver them. God's answer: "I am who I am" (Ex 3:14). We're used to those words, but a moment's reflection leaves us wondering what that name means. God does not tell Moses to say to Israel that God is powerful or wise or gracious; instead, he must tell Israel that God claims the *fact of existence*. "I am" means: "I exist". The additional words, "who I am", expands on the first words to state: I exist as I exist. Enslaved Israelites must know that this God claims *fullness* of existence, that all existence is in him. In Jesus' words: "the Father has life in himself" (John 5:26). So the Israelites in Egypt derive their existence from him (as is true for all creatures), be it today or tomorrow. There is such richness of being in God that nothing can add to him (as if to improve him). His fullness of being means instead that it can only go the other way around, ie, that he enriches others, that all things get their existence from him. In Paul's words, "For from him and through him and to him are all things," Rom 11:36; cf 1 Cor 8:6. Hence Bavinck's memorable phrase: God is an "unbounded ocean of being". Such perspective concerning God is so encouraging for Egyptian slaves as they receive a promise of their upcoming deliverance.

This understanding of God as fullness of being (and hence source of all that exists) explains why Paul can tell the people of Athens that God "is not served by human hands, as though he needed anything, since he himself gives to all mankind life and breath and everything", Acts 17:25. God *is* life, is *fullness* of life, and so life travels *from* him, not *to* him as if he needed anything from us (cf Ps 50:9ff). This contrasts with Demetrius' words about the goddess Artemis when he said that losing worshippers would result in her being "deposed from her magnificence" (Acts 19:27). The implication is that her magnificence depended on her being worshipped, ie, she

---

10 Note that the *Belgic Confession* as printed in the *Book of Praise* provides no Scripture references beside the word "simple". That's because the doctrine of God's simplicity does not rest on one or more explicit prooftexts but is the necessary conclusion of reading all Scripture – just as the Trinity. Similarly, the term "simple" in relation to God is not found in the Bible – just like the word Trinity.

needs people in order to be who she is (something true of all idols). But eternal God does not need people in order to be who he is since he has fullness of existence, life, in himself.

Prism

Yet God has revealed concerning himself that he *has* infinitude, wisdom, omniscience, and so many other attributes (some of which are listed in Article 1). He also revealed that he *is* life, love, spirit, truth, etc. These various terms reveal the fullness of his being. He is not *part* wisdom and *part* love and *part* truth, etc, but the fullness of his existence manifests itself as wisdom and love and omniscience and faithfulness, etc. Similarly, he does not *have* wisdom or love or kindness one moment so as to *not have* these aspects another moment. Rather, these various qualities of God are in him one and the same and therefore constant. But we creatures are too finite to grasp such a thing because we of necessity differentiate; in our creaturely world *this* cannot be *that*. So God has condescended to let us see multiple angles of his fullness, so that one time we see his wisdom, another time his love, another his goodness, etc. So perhaps a better earthly analogy than car or body (ie, parts) might be the concept of light. There is a singleness in light, yet run through a prism light refracts into multiple colours, and one sees different colours depending on the angle of the refraction. God is simple and always the same. But as we look upon him (as revealed in his Word and works), we see different colours, qualities, aspects belonging to him (be it wisdom, goodness, truthfulness, etc). And so we are prompted to marvel at his immeasurable *God*ness – and we're left searching for fitting words to capture his blessed identity.

How is this Important?

Perhaps you say: for daily life this sounds like a lot of ado about very little; surely there are more important things to talk about than the complicated simplicity of God. Maybe. I for one, though, am deeply grateful the term "simple" is in our confession about God. I'd like to draw out a few implications of this rich term as they touch on our lives in this world.

In the first place, this single word "simple" provides the answer to that unhappy development in our modern North American world connected to *panentheism*. For reasons that need not now detain us, there's a stream of thought gaining traction that describes the relation between God and his people as *mutually interactive*.[11] To be more precise, this line of thinking suggests that God and man can -and do- mutually *influence* each other. As there is a to-ing and fro-ing in human interaction such that Bobby can influence Billy (eg, awaken a smile in a grumpy mood; conversely, destroy Billy's happiness with an insensitive remark), so people can influence God, affect his 'mood' and generate a response. Think of the concept of bargaining with God, promising to do this or that for God IF he fulfils a particular wish for you.

Among people a pledge to *do this or that* may be a winsome way to extract something desirable from the other. But God's *simplicity* means that he has no needs – and so we have no lever to extract anything from him. He has fullness of life in himself and so there is nothing we can offer him to twist his arm to our advantage. That makes the concept of mutualism unacceptable.

I need to take this thought a step further. Did God create mankind (and the rest of the world) because he needed us? We flatter ourselves to think that that might indeed be the case. But the simplicity of God -he has fullness of being in himself- excludes that possibility. He did not create this world so that this world might *add* something to him. He did not create this world either so that *he* might add something to himself. He *is* life, infinite fullness of being, unlimited richness of existence – and so cannot grow or expand or improve. All existence (and every facet of it) flows from God to the creature and nothing flows in the other direction to satisfy a lack in God. But if that is so, then Adam on the day of his creation could not claim any sense of entitlement, as if there was something in himself that God needed. Since life came fully from God alone Adam could never earn anything from God or position himself in such a way that God owed him something. Rather, from the start Adam existed by God's grace alone. With the fall into sin this grace received a deeper

---

11 See James Dolezal, *All that is in God*,

dimension, for God from his infinite fullness gave his Son to redeem sinners. And he did so not so that the redeemed might add anything to God, but he did so because he was *pleased* to do so, cf Eph 1:4ff.

This presses on us today the lesson that we may not in any way think that God needs us, nor are we to search for ways to get him over the barrel to owe us one. His simplicity excludes every sense of entitlement. On the contrary, he only *gives* from his fullness so that creatures may be augmented. So we major in augmenting others also.

Secondly (and connected to the first), God's simplicity means that we cannot *influence* God negatively. A cranky child is likely to awaken irritation in an exhausted mother because of her need for sleep. Anyone who sings songs to a heavy heart annoys the hearer. But God never has a need such that we annoy or irritate him – or lift his spirits. Since he has no needs, he is utterly beyond being influenced. The glorious gospel of that truth is that he does not get irritated by my weaknesses and sins so as to hit out at me in a temper. Given how weak and sinful I am, that's truly good news. The abundance of life he has in himself prompted him to give his only Son to atone for my sin so that he might adopt me as his child – O glorious gospel! I need not fear that he has regrets on having shared so much life with me!

Of course, we all know that the Bible mentions in various places that human activity prompted sorrow in God. We read in Gen 6:6 that "the Lord regretted that he had made man on the earth"; in 1 Sam 15:11 that "I regret that I have made Saul king"; in Ex 32:14, in response to Moses' intercession in the episode of the golden calf that "the Lord relented of the disaster that he had spoken of bringing on his people"; in Jonah 3:10 that "God relented of the disaster that he had said he would do to [Nineveh], and he did not do it". In these cases (and others) we are again confronted with God's anthropomorphic manner of speaking. Since God is above time, there is with him no *before* and *after*, no *now* and *then*. Yet these texts speak of God's response *after* he'd observed a human action. For us to understand something of God's hatred of sin or something of his boundless mercy in the face of repentance he condescends to speak in human language of "regret" and "relent", and categories of *before* and *after*. We definitely need to embrace the reality of our responsibility before God and how God responds to our transgressions. But we're not to think that God's "moods" depend on human stimulation as if we can touch God in his temperament or enrich him or impoverish him. To say it all in other terms: God had determined from eternity not to destroy Nineveh but to use Jonah to prompt the needed repentance; God had determined from the start to remove Saul from the kingship and install David; God had determined never to destroy Israel and start a new covenant people from Moses' descendants. Actions on earth never catch God by surprise; he ordains all things so that all things come from his hand (see Job 42:11; Amos 3:6; Mt 10:29f). But at the end of the day we simply cannot exercise an influence upon God. Thankfully!

In third place, God's simplicity means that there is no space for us to play one quality of God out against another quality. To our finite way of thinking, there is a tension between God's mercy on the one hand and his justice on the other[12], or between his love and his hate, his goodness and his wrath. After all, *this* cannot be *that*. But within God there is no tension between *this* and *that* because in him they are one and the same, ie, *God's* colour is love and goodness and mercy to his creatures, and wrath and justice and hate when his love and goodness and mercy are spurned. Hate does not cancel God's love but is an expression of his love-spurned. Wrath does not appear when his mood is sour (his mood is unchanging – if in fact we can speak of 'moods' in God) but is the expression of his love-snubbed.

Fourth, we read in the Bible of terms like good or wise or lovely or evil, etc. Our natural inclination is to load such like terms with human definitions. What's "good", for example, is what makes us feel good; what's "wise" is what makes sense to us, etc. But if life itself comes from God (since he is fullness of life), our definitions need to come from God. Something is "good" not because we like it but because it reflects God's goodness; something is "wise" or "lovely"

---

12 In LD 4 the *Heidelberg Catechism* even seems to foster this tension with its statement that God "will punish [our sins] by a just judgment," and then ask: "But is God not also merciful?" To which the Catechism gives this answer: "God is indeed merciful, but he is also just".

or "evil" not because we think it to be so, but because it reminds of the colour we see as God's fullness is refracted in the prism of God's activity. Paul writes that "for those who love God all things work together for good" (Rom 8:28). The fact that God is "simple" implies that we need to load that word "good" according to who God is. *His* definition of "good" involves that he would mold us through the things he puts on our path to reflect ever more accurately who he is – as the apostle indicates in the next verse, "… to be conformed to the image of his Son."[13]

Fifth, God does not need our worship. He does not need our service either. That's a humbling thought. It's also an essential thought inasmuch as awareness of this reality affects our motive for worshipping and hence our manner. We do not worship him to enlarge him or to improve him. Rather, we worship him to praise him for the overflowing abundance he has generously poured out on sinners in Jesus Christ and so to magnify his reputation in the eyes of other creatures. If the motive for worship is gratitude (and not addition), then the manner will be only what's consistent with his greatness. Our tastes are irrelevant; his life-giving greatness is everything.

Beyond…

I do not pretend to understand the simplicity of God; it's too *divine* for my finite mind to grasp. Perhaps that's also why this item of doctrine doesn't have much profile amongst Christians. Yet we do well to continue to try to appreciate that our Father in Jesus Christ is an "unbounded ocean of being", limitless in richness of being. With such a Father we never lack – neither in this life or the life to come.

---

13 With appreciation to Jason vanVliet in Clarion, Nov 2022.

God is holy – how AWESOME is that?!

The previous two chapters of this brief publication sought to supply an antidote to how we actually perceive God in the course of our average decision-making processes. God, we commonly feel, is somewhat distant from our actual circumstances and quite willing to bend some rules to accommodate our happiness. As a corrective to that thought, I suggested, God's *love* is so deep that he seeks to *enrich* the unworthy and undeserving – so who would want such a God at arm's length?! Further, his *simplicity* implies that he is constant in his being, an unbounded ocean of existence from whom we receive all we need for a life of fullest pleasure – so we have every reason to feel confident in his abundance.

With this present chapter (and the next) we edge back a step to consider God's *God*ness without the restraints of our deistic and panentheistic leanings. I think it necessary to do so because our western culture has subjected God to a process of -let me call it- *creaturisation*. The point of the term is that the Creator has been reduced to the level and ability of a finite creature. Devout Christians invariably inhale the air of today's spiritual climate and so are unavoidably infected by this reductionistic virus, together with its inescapable fallout. I would suggest that the vaccine against this virus is a renewed appreciation for the *holiness* of God.[14]

---

14 Peels, *Heilig is Zijn naam*, p. 20.

Guido deBrès in his *Belgic Confession* makes no mention of God's holiness, neither in the article where he lists the attributes of God (Article 1) nor anywhere else in his Confession. The closest he comes is in describing the Trinity at "holy" (2x in Article 9, once in Article 11). He does, however, use the term "holy" as a descriptive adjective in relation to numerous things, eg, holy Scripture, holy will, holy prophets, holy works, life, faith, places, congregation, church, assembly, ordinance, supper, signs, sacraments. In so doing deBrès follows the pattern of Scripture. The Bible uses the term "holy" several times in relation to God, eg, Josh 24:19: "You are not able to serve the Lord, for he is a *holy* God"; Is 6:3: "holy, holy, holy"; and more than two dozen times in Isaiah alone (and scarcely elsewhere) we read the phrase "the Holy One of Israel". Nevertheless, Scripture much more often uses the term in relation to holy *things*, eg, "holy ground", Ex 3:5; "holy place" in tabernacle, Ex 26:33f; "holy garments" for priests, 28:2,4; holy oil, coat, house, field, etc. Items on this earth are "holy" never of themselves nor ever because they have some sanctifying effect on God but always because holy God has a particular effect on these things. That's a vital point: in Scripture holiness is always centred in God and travels from God to creatures; never the other way around.

What does the term mean??

To today's North Americans, the term "holy" or "holiness" carries with it a sense of prudishness, stuffiness, strictness, moral purity; it smacks of God not wanting people to have any fun in life and so belongs in the same unpleasant category as *law*. That is simply *not* the Biblical loading of the term.

The Hebrew term behind the English word "holy" is שודק – qadosh. Linguists agree that the Hebrew term behind the English word "holy" means "to cut". What you "cut" away is separated from its original, made distinct, different. Applied to God, the term means that God is unique, in a class by himself. That is not at all surprising, for all reality fits in one of two categories: Creat*or* and Creat*ed*. The Creator is of necessity more than what he created, *above* his creatures, *Other, Separate, Distinct, Unique*. That's what's communicated in the word "holy". In his Confession deBrès hints at this *Otherness* of God

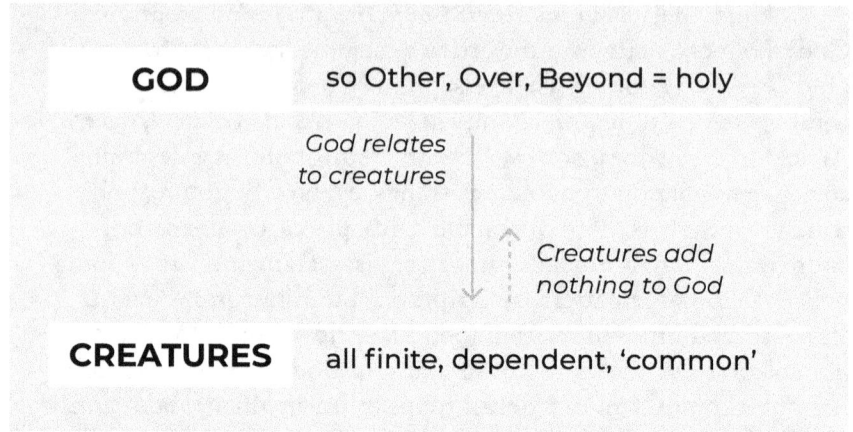

with his use of terms as "eternal" and "incomprehensible". Inhabitants of the category *Created* can never get their creaturely heads around the lone Inhabitant of the category *Creator*.

Yet here's a wonderful marvel: this God-in-the-Other-category has reached into the category of creatures to initiate and maintain a *relationship*[15]. In that relationship he remains Creator and Sustainer (Distinct, Other, ie, holy) and he causes creatures to remain creatures, dependent. Creatures are touched by his holiness, his Otherness and so enriched; he is not touched by our mundaneness so as to become impoverished.

Second Commandment

We receive a practical outworking of the Lord's uniqueness, distinctiveness, or otherness in the second commandment. The Lord expressly forbade his people from making "a carved image or any likeness of anything that is in heaven above or that is in the earth beneath, or that is in the water under the earth" (Ex 20:4). He motivated his prohibition with his self-revelation that he was "a jealous God".

---

15 Bavinck, II, 216ff.

2ND Commandment – no images

Not molten:	Not mental:
Bull	Like demanding father
Fish	Like friendly neighbour
Man	Like angry creditor

The point of this ban on images is that in the category called Created there is no creature able to represent adequately what God is like. Israel's construction of a calf in Ex 32:4 failed to capture the identity of the Creator, as did also Dagon of the Philistines or Baal of the Canaanites, etc. This God is *different*, unique, incomparable to anything in the category *created* – holy. So his earthly residence in the Most Holy Place of the tabernacle was … empty[16]. Yes, there was an ark in the Most Holy Place representing God's throne, but seated on this throne was … nothing. Better said: what was there -God- was beyond creaturely ability to discern. His *holiness,* his Otherness, his Uniqueness precluded the possibility of an image.

Of course, we could fashion an image of God in more ways than with a chisel. Beside physical -say, molten- images it's also possible to generate a *mental* image of God. Job's friends had a humanized perception of God so that they attributed human attitudes and logic to God. Their argument to Job was that God would not put evil on his path unless Job deserved it – a very human way of thinking (which required repentance, cf Job 42:7). The fourth friend, Elihu, was on the right track when he rebuked them with his insistence that "God is greater than man", Job 33:12; cf 34:13ff; 37:22ff. In his own words to Job the Lord made clear that he was in a category all by himself, and so beyond human, creaturely comprehension, Job 38-42. It's the concept of *different, other, holy.*

---

16 Cf Peels, p. 8.

Isaiah

Tragic though it is, we cannot be surprised that Israel's history saw repeated efforts to humanize (or creaturise) heaven's holy Inhabitant. The prophet Isaiah says in 1:4 concerning Israel: "They have forsaken the Lord, they have despised the Holy One of Israel, they are utterly estranged." Yet what's so amazing is that the people of Israel were deeply pious. Later in this same chapter we read about "the multitude of your sacrifices" and "burnt offerings of rams" and "the fat of well-fed beasts" (v. 11) as well as "many prayers" (v. 15). What was it, then, that prompted God to fault Israel for forsaking him? This: they fashioned a mental image of God so as to humanize him in the sense that God was surely pleased with all their contributions to his service just as people would be pleased by receiving many gifts. The king himself set the example. In his devotion to the Lord -and he was a devout man, cf 2 Chron 26:4f- he considered it fitting that he enter the temple of the Lord himself to burn incense (which represents prayer) on the altar of incense, cf 2 Chron 26:16. This was an activity that God had expressly granted only to priests. But the king had in his mind an image of God that allowed for more relaxed tolerance on God's part in response to his service to God. For his sin of serving God as he himself thought appropriate, the Lord struck him with leprosy.

In the same year that this king died, the Lord made it his business to press upon Israel -again- what his holiness, his Otherness, his Uniqueness really means, cf Is 6:1. He permitted Isaiah to see a vision of the Lord which the prophet was to record and share with the people – for their instruction. The prophet records his vision in these words:

> *¹In the year that King Uzziah died I saw the Lord sitting upon a throne, high and lifted up; and the train of his robe filled the temple. ²Above him stood the seraphim. Each had six wings: with two he covered his face, and with two he covered his feet, and with two he flew. ³And one called to another and said:*
>
> "*Holy, holy, holy is the Lord of hosts;
> the whole earth is full of his glory!*"

> *⁴And the foundations of the thresholds shook at the voice of him who called, and the house was filled with smoke. ⁵And I said: "Woe is me! For I am lost; for I am a man of unclean lips, and I dwell in the midst of a people of unclean lips; for my eyes have seen the King, the Lord of hosts!"*
>
> *⁶Then one of the seraphim flew to me, having in his hand a burning coal that he had taken with tongs from the altar. ⁷And he touched my mouth and said: "Behold, this has touched your lips; your guilt is taken away, and your sin atoned for."*

What did Isaiah see? He writes: "I saw the Lord" – then proceeds to tell us nothing of what the Lord looked like but focuses instead on the chair upon which the Lord was sitting. That chair was "a throne, high and lifted up." We understand that a "throne", though more elaborate and decorated than a normal chair, remains a chair of common size for the average 6-foot person. So its seat is about 1½ feet above the ground and its legs spaced about 1½ feet apart. But the chair upon which the prophet sees the Lord seated is "high and lifted up" – its seat way above the ground, its one leg on this hill and another on the other side of yonder hill – BIG. That's the only thing that catches Isaiah's attention concerning the chair; it's *huge*. That says something about the *otherness* of God!

Further, "the train of his robe filled the temple." We're accustomed to a bride's dress having a train perhaps measuring a few feet. The train of the Lord's robe was of such magnitude that it "filled the temple". The Holy Place was some 40 x 15 feet (and the Most Holy Place 15 feet square). With his train filling it, we're to picture the table and the incense altar blanketed by the train – and hence Isaiah himself squeezed out. In relation to a church, we might say that his train filled the aisle, covered the pews, overlaid the organ, etc. The point is not that the Lord was excessively tall but that his Godness was so overwhelming as to leave no space unfilled.

Above him stood seraphim, angels. The term "seraph" comes from the Hebrew word for *burning*. There is something so *Other* about God that these angels-in-his-presence catch fire (recall the bush of Ex 3 burning at God's presence and Mt Sinai catching fire when God descended, Ex 19). Though these angels were created to be ever in God's presence, they never got used to his nearness but each "covered his face" – clearly indicating that the Otherness of his Godness (his brightness?) was *too much* for their creaturely (though angelic) eyes to behold. Similarly, they covered their feet in his presence as symbol of their creatureliness and humility. With their final two wings they "flew" in immediate obedience to God's instructions, cf Ps 103:21f; Heb 1:14.

All the while they called non-stop: "Holy, holy, holy…" = Unique, Unique, Unique; Different, Different, Different; Other, Other, Other; Separate…; this God is *unlike* anything else in all creation. To Isaiah as observer that endless song would surely be self-evident given the size of the chair and the magnitude of his train, to say nothing of the angels' burning and their covered faces and feet. As the prophet himself said later: "To whom then will you liken God?!" (40:18; cf v. 25; 46:5). There is absolutely nothing in the category of *Created* that supplies a fitting comparison to the *Creator*. Truly unique, *Other!*

The prophet hears the rest of the seraphim's song: "the whole earth is full of his glory". The term "earth" is that part of God's creation where Isaiah lives. The term "glory" captures the idea of weightiness, impressiveness, gravitas – in this case clearly the gravitas of God's holiness. The thought is that as his train fills the temple, his Otherness -the *outflow* of his holiness/uniqueness[17]- fills his entire creation. Every part of God's creation is loaded with the evidence of his Uniqueness, his world overflows with his Otherness. If he is *Too-much* for the seraphim to observe, how much more is that so for creation – and so we're not surprised to read that the foundations of the thresholds of the temple shook at the voices of these angles calling back and forth of his holiness, uniqueness, distinctness (see also Ps 29:8f). Similarly, we're not surprised to read that "the house

---

17 Vos, *Redemptive History and Biblical Interpretation* (Presbyterian & Reformed, 1980), pg 280: "Closely connected with the conception of holiness is that of the divine Kabod or glory. The latter is the outward manifestation of the former. Glory is revealed holiness in the metaphysical as well as in the ethical acceptance of the term."

was filled with smoke" – for God "is a consuming fire" (Dt 4:24; Heb 12:29), as the seraphim illustrate.

Humility

It all raises a question. Why did Isaiah not provide us with a description of God himself?? He says he "saw the Lord", v. 1, and then gives us only a description of *creaturely stuff around him*. Why?

Surely it is self-evident that Isaiah's (creaturely) eyes *could not focus* on God! If heavenly angels (the seraphim) covered their faces in the presence of God, what would happen to Isaiah's eyes if he were to look at this Holy One?!! God himself had once told Moses: "you cannot see my face, for man shall not see me and live" (Ex 33:20; cf Judg 6:22f; 13:22). Similarly, the man Isaiah could not find words to describe God adequately; human, creaturely vocabulary is too finite, too limited, to capture the identity, the essence, of God. Recall the concept of *anthropomorphism* as described in the previous chapter.

God is simply too *Other*, too *different*, too *unique* for any creature to grasp. So we are not to even try to get a picture in our heads of who he is, ie, no molten image and no mental image. For he is absolutely unique, fully in a class by self. No creaturely comparisons will suffice to capture his distinctive uniqueness.

The fact that we can never grasp him drives home the need for deep *humility* on our part in relation to him. Joshua's words to Israel are essential: "you are not able to serve the LORD, for he is a holy God" (Josh 24:19; cf Job 33:6) – too unique, too other, too different for creatures to worship. How dare we -like Job's friends- think that we can master him, describe him, get him straight in our heads, serve him… He is infinitely *beyond* us. As deBrès put it in Article 1 of his *Belgic Confession*: he is *incomprehensible* to creatures (and sinners at that).

This, of course, makes his condescension, his willingness to relate to us, all the more miraculous and marvellous! Though he remains *God, Other, Too-much*, he yet connects with creatures (sinners!) – to the point of making such creatures his children. There are no words to adequately capture the glory, the gravitas, the splendour of such kindness!

When it dawned on Isaiah who God really was, it also dawned on him who *he* was. "Woe is me!" was Isaiah's broken response, "for I am lost; for I am a man of unclean lips…," v. 5. It's actually a striking response, for we half expect some expression of "Wow!!" But there is no wow-factor here; there is only a humility-factor, an expression of utter self-lostness in the face of the presence of such Otherness, such Uniqueness, such holiness, such *God*ness. If heavenly seraphim burst into flame in the presence of this God, how much more should earthly Isaiah perish in his fire!

Grace

Here is again the wonderful *Otherness* of this God: he sent a burning seraph with a coal snatched from the temple's altar. The altar of the temple, of course, stood between the Most Holy Place in the back of the temple where God dwelt and the people outside; he was too holy for creatures to approach, and sinners were too vile to enter the proximity of God. The sacrifices on that altar, then, foreshadowed the work of the coming Lamb of God, Jesus Christ, to atone for sin. Well now, that symbol of Christ's work must cleanse the prophet so that his sin would not trigger his demise in the face of God's holiness. This, we realize, is the good news of God's grace.

Impossible challenge

Now that God has revealed something of his radical *Too-muchness*, his Otherness, he asks for a volunteer to tell this material to his people-by-covenant – the same people who "despised the Holy One of Israel" (1:4), who trample the courts of his temple with their sacrifices (1:11ff) while at the same time ripping off the poor, loving bribes, and crushing the widows (1:21ff); to them God was so … normal, creaturely, nice… Isaiah is so taken by this vision of God's Otherness that he instantly volunteers: "Here I am! Send me!" (6:8).

Perhaps we appreciate his zeal to share what God's holiness really means. But *this* God quickly poured cold water on the prophet's zeal. Though they'd hear all about the vision Isaiah saw, their shrunken perception of God would prevent them from grasping the significance of his *holiness* (6:9f). Instead, their insistence of worshipping God as if he remained their kind of creature would land them one day in exile, spewed from the land of Promise (6:11f; cf Dt 28:15ff). The one redeeming prospect for his corrupt people would be a "holy seed" (v. 13), a *different* seed, *a unique* seed. That, we realize, is a reference to Jesus Christ.

Jesus Christ

As the prophet Isaiah carries out his mandate to show the people of Israel who God is, he must also relate the words of Isaiah 53:2f:

"...he had no form or majesty that we should look at him,
and no beauty that we should desire him.
He was despised and rejected by men,
a man of sorrows, and acquainted with grief;
and as one from whom men hide their faces
he was despised, and we esteemed him not."

The passage has such a different texture than the picture of Isaiah 6; there is here no majesty, no otherness at all. Here is simply broken humanity, to the point of being offensive. Yet there is a striking parallel: as the seraphim of Isaiah 6 deliberately covered their faces so as not to look at God, so here "men hide their faces" so as not to see the despicable man Isaiah is talking about.

That parallel makes the juxtaposition of these two texts in John 12 so striking. In John 12:38, John quotes Is 53:1: "Lord, who has believed what he heard from us, and to whom has the arm of the Lord been revealed?" Then two verses later (v. 40) he quotes Is 6:10: "He has blinded their eyes and hardened their heart, lest they see with their eyes, and understand with their heart, and turn, and I would heal them." We need to add: when NT writers quote from the OT, they typically intend their quote to awaken in the minds of their readers not simply the literal words quoted but the entire passage from which the quote is lifted. John, then, is setting side by side not simply two verses but two *chapters*, two visions about God – one highlighting his holiness, his otherness, his uniqueness; the other highlighting his plainness, his humility, his despicability. Then -surprise!- John adds this comment: "Isaiah said these things because he *saw his glory…*," John 12:41.

His *glory*: that's the *outflow of his holiness*, that's the Creator's Otherness expressing itself in this creaturely world. That is: Jesus was the fulfilment of the Otherness, the Holiness of Is 6 *and* he was the fulfilment of the misery and despicability of Is 53.[18] In Jesus Christ God displayed his Otherness, his Differentness in radical fashion: *in the Son the Creator went to the cross to redeem creatures!* That's awesome, that's glorious; we can't find sufficient words to capture how *wonderful* this is! Christ-on-the-cross: how despicable, how other, how holy, how unique, how awesome; we have seen his glory, glory as of the only Son from the Father, full of grace and truth (John 1:14). God the Creator in the flesh, the Holy One of Israel as a creature, to atone for sin!

This same Creator is today present in his created world through his Holy Spirit. Through the Spirit he is pleased to relate to sinners, to live with sinners in an absolutely unique, out-of-this-world fashion – eternal God in human hearts; no wonder the Bible calls him the *Holy* Spirit! The marvellous result is that creatures become temples of God the *holy* Spirit (1 Cor 3:16) and transformed so as to image (!) something of God's Otherness; people are so *sanctified* as become different, separate, unique-from-this-world, cf Lev 11:44; 1 Peter 1:16: "You shall be holy, for I am holy". So even the utensils of life become holy, unique, set apart (cf Zech 14:20; Ex 28:36-38). The common and normal become special, different, holy, not because 'common' things point to someone divine, but because God takes the 'common' and ordains them for his service.

Implications

God's identity as *Other, Different, Unique*, so *beyond* creaturely comprehension dictates a number of consequences.

---

18 John Piper, www.desiringgod.org/messages/in-the-throne-room

Implications

1.	Resist mental images!
2.	Beware criticizing God's deeds
3.	*Adoration*
4.	Holy lifestyle 24/7

The first relates to our impulse to make a mental image of God. It comes so easy to us to think that we have God's measure, that we've figured out what keeps God happy, how we can serve him in a way that ensures his smile upon us. In step with our western context, we embrace a concept of God that highlights his love and compassion and kindness (understood humanly), and that's what we enjoy hearing about. Conversely, we disdain hearing about his wrath, his jealousy, his hatred (again, understood humanly). Predictably, preferring such messages leads to the sort of conduct Isaiah criticized: while there was plenty of church going, plenty of voluntary contributions, plenty of prayers (all when it suits), there was simultaneously deep neglect of caring for the oppressed, of true justice for the weak, of emptying self to serve another, of being aware that I'm always in the presence of such a *glorious* God. The words of the prophet Micah, Isaiah's contemporary, are instructive: "What does the Lord require of you but to do justice, and to love kindness, and to walk humbly with your God"? (Mic 6:8). Yet failing to walk that way is invariably what happens when we reduce him to our size, when we humanize God, when we extrapolate our preferred emotions onto him. God's revelation concerning his utter *holiness* is the necessary corrective to this creaturisation of God.

The second relates to our tendency to complain about what sovereign God has put on our path. We protest to God (whether directly to his face or indirectly in our thoughts and conversations) that how he's dealt with us is unfair, that we deserve a better deal. But in such criticism, we have in our thinking brought God down from his exalted Otherness to the level of a discussion partner, as if the Holy

One owes us an explanation for his sovereign deeds. Elihu showed the better way: "I too was pinched off from a piece of clay" (Job 33:6). God is so *Other* than I, so unique, so different -holy!- that it is not for me to push back against God, to protest his deeds in my life. It is instead for me to submit with humility to what he in wisdom places on my path. My tendency to criticize God needs repentance.

In third place, his holiness, his otherness demands our adoration. Think about it: the infant who lay in the crib of Bethlehem was *God himself*; the Creator was pleased to become a creature, dependent on a mother pinched off a piece of clay for a feed and to have his diaper changed! The very thought is so *other* from what we people would suggest, so *unique*, so *holy* as to be beyond our imagination. Similarly: the reject hanging on the cross of Calvary was *God* the Son who'd come to atone for rebels' sins. How incomprehensible to the human mind, how bizarre, how *other, unique, different* from what we people would expect or do. But this is God -holy- and so infinitely worthy of adoration.

Fourth, in his Holy (!) Spirit this God has come to dwell in our hearts; "do you not know that you are God's temple and that God's Spirit dwells in you?" (1 Cor 3:16). It follows that "as he who called you is holy, you also be holy in all your conduct" (1 Peter 1:15). The child of God is called to be different, other, unique, separate in this world; in this world but not *of* this world – and to be content with being out of sync with the majority around us. The blessed identity of our Father in Jesus Christ is the root of all Christian ethics and the catalyst for the Christian's holy lifestyle.

God is *Al*mighty: What does *Al* mean?

Of all the attributes of God listed in Article 1, that of his being *almighty* is undoubtedly one of the more familiar. We do, after all, confess every week anew with the Apostles' Creed: "I believe in God the Father *almighty*, Creator of heaven and earth." Or with the Nicene Creed: "We believe in one God, the Father *almighty*, Maker of heaven and earth, of all things visible and invisible."

We also, I suspect, feel capable of providing somewhat of an explanation of what the term seeks to confess. Attached as the word is to the concept of *creation*, we acknowledge readily that it takes <u>all-mighty</u> God to fashion this world out of nothing, simply through a word of command, from the *macro* of seemingly endless galaxies to the *micro* of the complexities of how a cell is built and functions. We'd go further and readily acknowledge that maintaining and governing this complex world (think cyclones and earthquakes) requires almighty power.

Nevertheless, it seems to me that there is a disconnect between our understanding of what is confessed with the word *almighty* and the thought processes which actually happen in our heads in life's daily trials. As I was preparing the present lecture, a young man in my community died in a tragic car crash late at night. If the crash was the result of mechanical failure in his vehicle, could we say the Lord

God caused that failure? If he fell asleep, should we say the Lord gave him sleep? If there was black ice on the road (it was that time of year), would you say the Lord put that ice there? If he was dodging a raccoon, would you say the Lord had that raccoon cross the road just then? And what shall we say about the young man's possible split-second decisions about turning the wheel this way or that – was the Lord involved in that? We realize: to say that God is *al*mighty means that Yes, his hand was involved in each possibility; nothing comes by chance. But to our thinking that's too bold; doesn't that make the accident God's fault? And doesn't that mean there's no place left for free will?

I think it imperative that we face difficult questions as these head on. After all, we bump into these questions repeatedly on life's roads. Is a virus in God's hands? Do governments act by his will? Is the girl I married God's gift or my choice? Is God's hand in our civilization's embrace of euthanasia, abortion, gender fluidity, etc? What *does* AL-mighty mean??

Definition

We people all have some level of ability, of might and power to accomplish this or that; in fact, people are mightier than rabbits or flowers. As we speak of God's might -indeed, his *al*mighty power- the temptation is to extrapolate our human might to the nth degree and attach that concept to God. In that case God's almighty power is simply human might greatly enlarged.

God, though, is not a man -be it divinised- so that he fits in some way into our human categories. That he is *almighty* makes him essentially different from any creature this almighty God created. He is not *more than* finite mighty men; he is *above* all mights, all muscles, all powers, all authorities.[19]

The Bible uses numerous names for God that point up his power. Terms as *El, Elohim, El Shaddai* and *Adonai* all point to his power. Of particular significance is the term that's used some 280

---

19 vanGenderen, *Beknopte Gereformeerde Dogmatiek*, 177. See also Bavinck, *RD*, II,246ff.

times in the Old Testament: the LORD *of hosts*. The term pictures him as commander over limitless heavenly armies who accomplish his divine purposes – almighty. That concept is echoed in the New Testament with a word as *Pantocrator* (literally: all-ruler; hence translated as Almighty), cf Rev 1:8. The Bible also recounts so many works he performed that display his omnipotent ability; think of his creating this world, the universal flood, the plagues in Egypt, the walls of water in the Red Sea, the manna with which he nourished his people in the desert. God in the person of Jesus multiplied loaves, healed lepers, walked on water, arose from the dead, ascended into heaven. Scripture would have us know that nothing is impossible for God, cf Gen 18:14; Luke 1:37.

Yet that last statement needs qualification. If nothing is impossible for God, can he make a rock so big that he can't lift it? Can he create a square circle? Or a two-sided triangle? The Lord himself has told us that there are some things he *cannot* do. Please hear that well: I'm not now referencing things that God has said he *will* not do; I'm saying that there are things God *is not able* to do. The Holy Spirit says through Paul that God "cannot deny himself", 2 Tim 2:13 (cf Tit 1:2; Num 23:19; 1 Sam 15:29; Heb 6:18). So God cannot implode himself or make himself to become non-God. He cannot create another God to be his equal. In a word, his *omnipotence* is infinite, limited only by his own nature. So: he can do whatever doesn't contradict his nature.[20]

What, then, do we mean by the term Almighty? With that term we confess that his power can never be depleted, or drained, or exhausted. Rather, eternal God has *infinite* stores of ability. Isaiah 40 helps us to understand the point.

Isaiah 40

Isaiah spoke the words of this chapter to a people about to go into exile to Babylon, cf 39:5f: "Hear the word of the LORD of hosts (note that title for God in this context!): Behold, the days are coming,

---

20 See Robert Morey, *Battle of the Gods*, pg 244; Bavinck, RD, II, 247.

when all that is in your house … shall be carried away to Babylon." For the godly on the streets of Jerusalem, this was devastating news. So Isaiah tells the people, "Behold, the Lord God comes with might and his arm rules for him" (40:10). He then moves on to provide five illustrations of the *might* of this God, as follows:

1. **Works**: v. 12: "Who has measured the waters in the hollow of his hand and marked off the heavens with a span, enclosed the dust of the earth in a measure…?"

    a. The reference to measuring water is not only to how many handfuls of liquid there are in Lake Ontario or the Pacific Ocean; the reference is also to God having made this world with just the right amount of water on the planet to maintain temperatures needed to support life.

    b. The reference to marking off the heavens with a span (= the distance between extremities of outstretched thumb and little finger) isn't simply to discover how far away the moon or sun might be from the earth; it's also a reference to positioning Planet Earth in just the right spot in our galaxy to get the optimum gravitational pull and temperature to sustain life.

    c. The dust in the atmosphere is not just a reference to the effects of a sandstorm; it refers also to the multiple particles of oxygen, nitrogen, viruses, etc, that we need to inhale to retain good health.

    Scientists acknowledge in relation to each of these scenarios that minute differences would challenge the ability of our planet to sustain life. The point: *behold your God!*

2. **Nations**: v. 15: "Behold, the nations are like a drop from a bucket…" To the people of Jerusalem in Isaiah's day the reference to "nations" awakened awareness of Egypt, Assyria, Babylon, all fearsome in their military and economic abilities – to say nothing of the reputation of the Assyrian army for its pillaging and raping of its victims. In fact, Assyria had recently taken the northern tribes into exile. The scary question was who might be next…

So notice how God relates to Assyria and Egypt and superpowers: to God they are no more than a drop hanging under a bucket. That's the comparison: *who really cares* about that drop under a pail of water – a drip like Assyria?? As the prophet says in v. 17: "all the nations are as nothing before him." *Behold your God!*

3. **World:** v. 22: "It is he who sits above the circle of the earth, and its inhabitants are like grasshoppers." Today there are some 8 billion of these grasshopper-like creatures on our planet, all jumping in this direction or that in our endless busyness. God sits enthroned far above all these people, greatly exalted over these insects with their endless chirping and jumping. The comparison with grasshoppers puts talented humanity in its place as *irrelevant in themselves* to the Sovereign on the throne. *Behold your God!*

4. **Great men:** v. 23f: God "brings princes to nothing, and makes the rulers of the earth as emptiness." Egypt's Pharaoh, Assyria's Sennacherib, Nebuchadnezzar, Alexander the Great, Genghis Khan, Napoleon, Mao, Hitler, Stalin: where are they today? At his time this God has flicked them away as so much "emptiness", breath. So what shall become of Mr Putin? Or of Mr Xi? Or Mr Biden? They are all but a breath…, tomorrow God will blow on them, and they will wither. *Behold your God!*

5. **Stars:** v. 26: "Lift up your eyes on high and see: who created these? He who brings out their host by number, calling them all by name…" There is something so humbling about tilting your head back to look up on a clear night. Our six feet of height feels so insignificant when earth disappears from view and we see the countless stars of the Milky Way stretching so far above us from horizon to horizon. Through the James Webb telescope the Lord God has let scientists see two galaxies merging 500 million light years away. And God says he calls each star by name – which is to say that he's enthroned *above* such galaxies and controls their every behaviour! Truly, *behold your God!*

What might Isaiah's point be in mentioning all this? Interspersed between these five displays of God's almighty power is the repeated question: "To whom then will you liken God?" cf vv. 18,25. The lesson: those two letters "al" in *al*mighty is comprehensive! This God -*our* God- is *omnipotent*, absolutely sovereign! In the words of v. 28: "The LORD is the everlasting God, the Creator of the ends of the earth. He does not faint or grow weary…" His *almighty power* is never depleted; he cannot run out of ability. For people about to experience the trauma of exile, this was encouraging news.

DeBrès

Many years later Guido deBrès sat in his prison cell awaiting the day of his execution. His crime: he had preached the gospel, namely, what this almighty God had done in Jesus Christ to ransom sinners to be his children. In his cell he wrote a letter to his wife:

> *"My very dear Catherine Ramon, my precious and most loved wife and sister in our Lord Jesus Christ… You know well enough that when you married me, you married a mortal man whose life was not sure for a single minute. Yet it has pleased our good God to give us about seven years together, and five children. If the Lord had wanted us to live together longer, He has the means to make it happen. But it is not His pleasure; so, His will be done and that be sufficient to you.*
>
> *Remember too, that it was not by chance that I fell into the hands of my enemies, but through the providence of my God…. My God, You have let me be born at a time and hour determined by You, and through all the time of my life You have preserved and protected me in the face of unimaginable dangers, and You have fully delivered. And now, if the hour has come in which I must leave this life in order to go to You, Your will be done….*
>
> *Especially forget not the honour which God has shown to you by having given you a man who was not only a minister of the Son of God, but also a man so esteemed and privileged by God that He honoured him with the crown of martyrdom. I am joyful and my heart rejoices. I lack nothing in all my troubles. I am filled with*

the over-flowing riches of my God.... I had never thought that God would be so merciful to a poor creature as I am....

Adieu, Catherine, my dear good friend...."

It's the promise of Is 40: 29,31 come alive: "He gives power to the faint, and to him who has no might he increases strength… They who wait for the LORD shall renew their strength; they shall mount up with wings like eagles; they shall run and not be weary; they shall walk and not faint."

We read what deBrès wrote and find something in his words we deeply admire. Here is a sense of confidence, the peace that comes with knowing that God our Father is almighty. We love what the same deBrès put to paper in our cherished *Belgic Confession*, Article 13:

"We believe that this good God, after he had created all things, did not abandon them or give them up to fortune or chance, but that according to his holy will he so rules and governs them that in this world nothing happens without his direction."

It's so comforting. The apostle Paul said it nicely with his rhetorical question: "If God [almighty!] is for us, who can be against us"? (Rom 8:31). We happily shout out the answer: no one!

Yet that same confession raises so many questions. Is it correct to say that God was involved in deBrès' arrest and eventual murder? Was God asleep at the wheel during World War 2 when millions were murdered in cold blood in Auschwitz? Where is God when unknown thousands submit themselves today to chemical or surgical mutilation in pursuit of peace due to gender dysphoria – to say nothing about the murder of millions of preborn children? What is the relationship between almighty God and evil? Or the devil?

To be honest, we think that in our efforts to defend God's goodness we need to separate God from evil. But to do so is too costly, for in the process we end up limiting his almighty power – somehow. Our confession about his omnipotence means we need to address the question of evil.

Satan

I'd like to consider this question by turning our focus to Job. To the best of our knowledge, Job never learned of the discussion that occurred between God and Satan such that God put all Job's abundant possessions in Satan's hand (Job 1:12). On a given day messenger after messenger arrived at Job's door to relate the total loss of his oxen and donkeys and their attending servants (1:14f), his sheep and their shepherds (v. 16), his camels and their riders (v. 17) and finally the collapse of his son's house that killed all his 10 children in one hit (v. 19). Job responded with these words: "The LORD gave, and the LORD has taken away; blessed be the name of the LORD" (v. 21). Lest we think Job was mistaken in attributing all this evil to the Lord, the Holy Spirit adds this comment: "In all this Job did not sin or charge God with wrong" (v. 22).

On another day Job's skin broke out in painful sores from top to toe. Again, to the best of our knowledge, Job did not know about Satan's challenge to God and the opportunities God gave to Satan. In response to his illness Job's wife advised him to "curse God and die" (2:9). To which Job replied: "You speak as one of the foolish women would speak. Shall we receive good from God, and shall we not receive evil?" (2:10). We find jarring that Job attributes his misfortune directly to God. But the Holy Spirit again affirms Job's correctness by telling us, "In all this Job did not sin with his lips" (2:10b). The clincher on the subject appears at the end of the book when the Spirit tells us that Job's siblings "comforted him for all the evil that *the* LORD had brought upon him" (42:11; my emphasis). This inspired statement underscores the uniform instruction of Holy Scripture: God's almighty power is so extensive that Satan and all evil are as fully under God's omnipotent control as anything else in God's vast world. Satan is a creature under God's feet.

But that raises another pressing question: doesn't this mean that God is responsible for evil? Are we meant to understand that Job's calamities -and potentially ours- are God's doing? How can we in our thinking absolve God of blame for Satan's evils and yet retain our confession concerning his *almighty* power?

Very instructive on this point is how God responds to Job's bitter complaint (voiced in ch 23f). In his response God does not explain the interplay between himself and Satan (or evil), but instead the Lord shows Job his majesty and might – and so Job's finiteness and puniness. God asks in Job 38:4: "Where were you when I laid the foundations of the earth?" And a verse later: "Who determined its measurements?" To say it in the words of Isaiah 40: were you there when I figured out the land-to-water ratio for Planet Earth? Did I need your advice in determining where exactly to position Planet Earth in the heavenly galaxies? *What are you, Job?* Or 38:24: "What is the way to the place where the light is distributed, or where the east wind is scattered upon the earth?" Job, can you regulate how much light there needs to be outside so that plants flourish? Can you figure out what spawns a Colorado Low and control exactly where the system will drop its moisture? Or 39:26: "Is it by your understanding that the hawk soars and spreads its wings toward the south"? That is: is the annual migration of birds in your hand? Job, *who are you?!* If you can't figure out these earthly things, how do you expect to get your head around the almighty God who sits enthroned far above the circle of the earth??

The lesson is so instructive for us. There is so very much in God's creation that mankind can understand and even in some small way control. But the more we learn, the more we realize how little we actually know of God's wide world. We're only 6 feet tall and we exist in this world for a mere 70 years or maybe 80. If the stuff of this planet repeatedly bamboozles us, how do we expect to get our heads around the almighty Creator and the interplay between him and evil?

No, the Lord never explained that interplay to Job for the simple reason that its answer is beyond Job's finite mind. It's beyond ours too. At the end of the book Job acknowledged that his demands for an explanation were not befitting a creature made of dust and so he adopted a posture of humility and repentance: "Behold, I am of small account... I despise myself and repent in dust and ashes" (40:4; 42:6). It's a posture we do well to emulate.

And in our Confession we do:

God is not the Author of the sins which are committed nor can he be charged with them. For his power and goodness are so great and beyond understanding that he ordains and executes his work in the most excellent and just manner, even when devils and wicked men act unjustly. And as to his actions surpassing human understanding, we will not curiously inquire farther than our capacity allows us. But with the greatest humility and reverence we adore the just judgments of God, which are hidden from us and we content ourselves that we are pupils of Christ, who have only to learn those things which he teaches us in his Word, without transgressing these limits.[21]

Free will

The reality of God's omnipotence raises another problem to our minds, namely, the logical conclusion that we must be robots, preprogrammed to act according to his almighty control. To our way of thinking, his omnipotence means we cannot have a free will – and if we don't have a free will God cannot rightly hold us responsible for our conduct (let alone consign sinners to hell).

In broad terms, the position most commonly held among North American evangelical Christians is that people certainly have a free will, ie, the capacity to make decisions free of (divine) coercion. God, it's suggested, has relinquished some of his almighty power so that he gives serious space for us to make decisions and then he interacts with what we have chosen to do. Some would even say that God cannot know ahead of time what we will do. The strong positive of this position is that emphasis is laid on human responsibility. The obvious negative, though, is that justice is not done to God's sovereignty. The question is: how do we do justice to both God's all-encompassing and almighty sovereignty and at the same time do justice of our full responsibility for our conduct?

Being the people we are, the temptation is to begin our thinking from *man's* side and then squeeze God's sovereignty (invariably compromised) into man's shape. Given, however, that God the Creator is the measure of all things, this starting point will never do. As creatures-under-God we and our human will have no meaning

---

21 *Belgic Confession*, Article 13.

unless we begin our efforts to understand the point with God. And Scripture is categorical that God's power is limitless so that he himself determines my thoughts, my words and my deeds – including items so insignificant as what socks I chose to wear this evening.

His means of doing so is through the normal decision-making processes that fill all our activities. Yet where someone chooses to sin, God is not responsible for that choice; and when someone chooses to obey God's command, the credit rightly does belong to God. That sentence, of course, needs further elaboration.

When God created humanity in the beginning, he made us able to obey him perfectly; there was no fault in man, cf Gen 1:31. God gave the command to guard and keep the Garden (Gen 2:15) and that's to say that mankind was able to make responsible decisions. He had, we would say, a *will free* to serve God faithfully as steward of his creation. Among the decisions the human race could make was one that concerned the tree from which God had forbidden eating – on pain of death, Gen 2:17. Implicit in that command was the possibility that mankind could freely choose to disobey God, ie, he was able to sin. Consider the chart below.[22]

Before Fall	**After Fall**	**Sanctified**	**Glorified**
Able to sin	Able to sin	Able to sin	
Able to not sin		Able to not sin	Able to not sin
	Not able to not sin		
			Not able to sin

To our shame the human race opted to sin. The result of the Fall was that our hearts were corrupted so that from now on we *want* only sin. Left free to do our own thing, we shall invariably satisfy our desires and so freely choose only what displeases God (cf John 8:44; Eph 2:2). A *free* will after the Fall will always choose in step with

---

22 Cf Sproul, *Chosen by God*, pg 42ff.

our inner identity as persons dead in sin; I do not have the ability to choose *not-sin*. Think of holding the steering wheel of a car on a hill without brakes. You have freedom to veer to the left or to the right, but you do not have the freedom to *not-go-downhill*.[23]

As a result of the powerful redeeming work of our Lord Jesus Christ (cf John 6:65; 6:44), the Holy Spirit renews the hearts of those for whom Jesus died. In the strength of the Spirit, these people are empowered to choose to not sin, for example, to decide not to pass on a piece of sensational gossip. Despite this renewing work, however, these sanctified saints have not yet reached the goal of perfection – and so they will from time to time talk past their mouth. Still, a Christian may not think that he will always choose only to sin. It is not until we are perfected in the coming Paradise that we will no longer sin.

From the above it is clear *why* a choice to disobey God's command is the sinner's full responsibility, for which he must give account and bear the punishment (be it in Christ). For though created to not sin, the sinner has chosen in Adam to become corrupt. To return to the earlier analogy, we chose to remove the brakes from our car. Obedience, on the other hand, must be credited to the Spirit of God because he renews the sinner's heart.

With the above, however, we have not answered the question of how sin could enter the perfect world of almighty God. No, the Lord was not sleeping at the helm. On the contrary, Satan's activities in the Garden happened as fully under God's sovereign watch as Satan's attack on Job. Our finite minds (sinful at that) are not able -as with the discussion on Job- to comprehend the works of almighty God on the day of Genesis 3 so as to be able to say: now I *get* the interplay between God and our Fall into sin. Here we need the same humility in the presence of the almighty as God required of Job.

Implications

Where does this leave us? God's revelation concerning his *almighty* power dictates that a posture of humility is imperative on

---

23 See further Article 14, *Belgic Confession*.

our part. We can in no way go toe to toe with God so as to be able to understand our sovereign Creator, be it in terms of physical might or in mental prowess. His ways are ever and always far beyond our reach, cf Is 55:8f. We creatures need to be okay with that.

The wonderful thing is that knowing our place *under* this God provides so much rest for restless souls. This God sits enthroned far above Canada, North America, this Planet – and to him all its people are as so many grasshoppers, Is 40:22. That means that the goings-on on this Planet are essentially nothing more than *Grasshopper News* – and why, O why, should I let *that* get me down?! Rather, "the Lord is the everlasting God, the Creator of the ends of the earth. He does not faint or grow weary; his understanding is unsearchable," Is 40:28. Planet Earth is fully in his almighty hand.

To his power there is no end – and *that's my Father in Jesus Christ!!*

The Fear of God

If my efforts in the previous five lectures were in any way successful, the attentive reader will have come away with a renewed appreciation for the infinite majesty, the unsurpassable holiness, the glorious *God*ness of our God. Repeatedly I drew attention to the historic confessional statement of Reformed churches around the world:

> *"We all believe with the heart and confess with the mouth that there is only one God, who is a simple and spiritual being; he is eternal, incomprehensible, invisible, immutable, infinite, almighty, perfectly wise, just, good, and the overflowing fountain of all good."*[1]

But, as I indicated repeatedly in the previous pages, it is one thing to affirm a paper copy of this confessional statement – and so group ourselves with the classical *Theists* of history. It's an altogether different thing to put this confession into *practice*. As I argued in the first lecture, reformed Christians are too often a blend of Deists and Panentheists. That's because the thought patterns occurring in our decision-making processes see God as remote from daily life yet interested in our happiness (Moral Therapeutic Deism); more, God adapts his rules to accommodate the ongoing development of our

---

1 *Belgic Confession*, Article 1. This confession was authored by Guido deBrès in 1561 and adopted by the Dutch churches that same decade. In ensuing years Dutch migrants have taken this confession with them around the world.

tastes. In short, in a very real way reformed Christians habitually think that we hold the steering wheel of our lives in our own hands and appreciate that God is here for us when we run into trouble. The four characteristics unpacked in the subsequent lectures sought to provide correctives to this habit in our modern thinking.

The previous lectures had already given some attention to the matter of why any of this is important. But the time has come to focus specifically on that topic. I'd like in this last lecture to focus on the Biblical theme of the *fear of God*. If God is *as much God* as the previous lectures have presented him to be, then *fearing this God* cannot be an altogether surprising response.

The Term

As we read the term "fear of God", we realize instinctively that the word "fear" is connected to the words "of God" in a different way than the previous terms were. In the phrase "the love of God", the word "love" is clearly a characteristic of God describing who God is and so how he relates to humanity; the phrase describes movement from God to us (in the form of "love"). The same is true in the phrase "the simplicity of God"; "simplicity" is a characteristic within God that impacts how he relates to humanity. But in the phrase "the fear of God", "fear" is not a quality within God that captures how he relates to us; "fear" is instead an attitude within people that describes how we relate to God (with "fear"). In short, the term "fear" describes movement from people to God, namely, our response to who God is.

Contrast?

We further notice that in the Bible the term "fear"[2] has, as we see it, contrasting meanings as it describes human relations to God. On the one hand, the word describes terror, fright, trembling, being scared of God. Adam admitted that when he heard God coming in the Garden after his fall into sin he was "afraid" (Hebrew: "fear";

---

2   The term appears some 435x in OT; 150x in NT – be it in relation to people or nature or events or God.

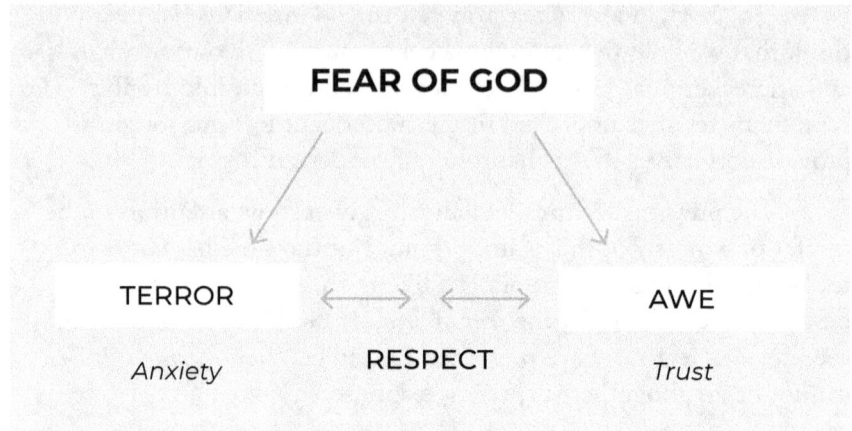

Gen 3:10). The author of the Letter to the Hebrews quotes Moses as saying at Mt Sinai, "I tremble with fear" (Heb 12:21). On the other hand, the word "fear" describes awe, reverence, veneration. David says in Ps 19:9 that "the fear of the LORD is clean" and in Ps 22:23: "You who fear the LORD, praise him!" We puzzle why the Lord God would use the same word for two seemingly opposing emotions.

We can untangle that riddle when we see how these two meanings of the term are opposite expressions of one and the same thing, viz, respect for God.³ With the term "respect" I mean the notion of *taking God seriously*. David once said concerning "the wicked" that "there is no fear of God before his eyes" (Ps 36:1). His point was that this segment of the human population does not take God seriously in their decision-making processes and so is content to plan evil. Such ignoring of God or denial of his Godness is the height of impiety and leads to unrestrained expression of the evil latent in human hearts.

---

3   See vanGemeren, W., ed. (1997). In *New international dictionary of Old Testament theology & exegesis* (Vol. 2, p. 528). Zondervan Publishing House.

But when one comes face to face with the reality of God's holy identity, you have no choice but to take him seriously. This *taking him seriously* moves in one of two directions. Noticing the *God*ness of God can lead a person on the one hand to a sense of deep terror (or fear); it can on the other hand lead a person to a profound sense of awe and adoration (or fear in the other sense). Whether the confrontation with God's *God*ness moves a person to terror or to adoration depends -might I say- on the observer's spiritual health.

Jonah

To illustrate, let's pause for a moment to look at the multiple ways the term "fear" is used in Jonah 1. The first use of the term appears in v. 5 to describe the sailors' response to the powerful storm the LORD had hurled upon the sea: "the mariners were *afraid*" (the Hebrew uses the word "fear" – וַיִּֽירְאוּ). At this point in the story the sailors have not yet been confronted with the LORD's Godness, for "each cried out to his [own] god," presumably for deliverance from the storm. Yet their terror for their safety was acute, because "they hurled the cargo ... into the sea."

The second appearance of the term "fear" occurs in v. 9, after the lot fell on Jonah. He says: "I am a Hebrew, and I *fear* the LORD, the God of heaven, who made the sea and the dry land" (יָרֵא). Though Jonah no doubt was also afraid of the storm and short on trust, the loading of the term this time moves in the direction of worship, ie, Jonah relates that he is a worshipper of the world's Creator (and hence almighty) – be it a lapsed worshipper. We note that Jonah's use of the term is simply to describe his religious affiliation and is devoid of action or emotion.

The term appears again in v. 10: "then the men were exceedingly *afraid*" – or, as the Hebrew has it, "feared a great fear" (וַיִּֽירְאוּ יִרְאָה גְדוֹלָה). This time the word "fear" denotes a deep terror, something more intense than the fear that prompted the sailors to throw their cargo overboard. For they have now come face to face with the almighty Creator God behind the storm – and seeing his *God*ness filled them with desperate terror.

Fear in Jonah 1

v. 5	the mariners were *afraid*
v. 9	I am a Hebrew, and I *fear* the LORD
v. 10	the men were exceedingly *afraid*
v. 16	the men *feared* the LORD exceedingly

TERROR ←————————————→ AWE

v. 10   v. 16
v. 5   v. 9

The final use of the term is in v. 16. After they had thrown Jonah overboard, the mariners noticed how the sea calmed instantly. "Then the men *feared* the LORD exceedingly, and they offered a sacrifice to the LORD…" (וַיִּֽירְא֧וּ יִרְאָ֛ה גְדוֹלָ֖ה) – again, "feared a great fear". But clearly the term "fear" this time denotes worship, as their offering a sacrifice to God demonstrates. The shift in the sense of the term "fear" in these verses is due to what the men experienced concerning the identity of the living God and so reflects what's happened in their hearts. They've moved from no respect for God (ie, not taking him seriously at all) to taking him seriously in deep terror to taking him seriously in worshipful adoration.

Mt Sinai

A second helpful illustration comes from the events as they unfolded at Mt Sinai. In the face of thunder and earthquakes and smoke and trumpet blasts, Moses told the people of Israel: "Do not fear (אַל־תִּירָאוּ), for God has come to test you, that the fear of him (יִרְאָתוֹ) may be before you, that you may not sin" (Ex 20:20). We notice that the word "fear" appears twice in this verse, the first time forbidding fear, the second time commanding fear. The first use angles in the direction of terror, being afraid, trembling, while the second moves through respect to something of worship. We notice too that the shift in nuance is due to what the Israelites had just witnessed, an experience so awesome that it necessarily bent the heart in the direction of worship (or at least, here, "that you may not sin").

But what was it that bent the people away from sin and into the direction of worship? Was it simply seeing smoke and fire and hearing the sound of thunder and trumpet and feeling the earth trembling?? Given all the displays of divine majesty which the Egyptians had experienced in recent months (cf Ex 7-11, 14) and the fact that these displays did not move them to worshipful adoration, that clearly cannot be the correct answer (see also Rev 6:12ff). There is something more going on here.

Note the words the Lord addressed to Israel through Moses *before* they experienced his visible and audible presence. He said: "You yourselves have seen what I did to the Egyptians, and how I bore you on eagles' wings and brought you to myself" (Ex 19:4). Three things stand out here:

- The reference to "what I did to the Egyptians" is a clear illusion to the devastation God inflicted upon the Egyptians through the ten plagues and their ultimate demise in the waters of the Red Sea. Clearly, God was to be *feared* – greatly, cf Ex 14:24.
- The words "how I bore you on eagles' wings" describes how the Lord God personally carried Israel above the fray -with no contribution on their part- so that the plagues did not hurt them and the waters of the Red Sea did not consume them. Here was mercy on God's part that had not been directed to the Egyptians.
- The words "and brought you to myself" refer specifically to the fact they are now physically *near* God and *not consumed* – again a marvellous display of mercy.

It is *after* these references to God's glorious mercy that he tells Moses that he's "coming … in a thick cloud", 19:9. Three days later "there were thunders and lightnings and a thick cloud on the mountain and a very loud trumpet blast, so that all the people in the camp trembled", because "the LORD had descended on it in fire", v. 16,18. The people did well to fear and keep their distance (vv. 21ff), yet God's earlier revelation of mercy made plain that he did not come as an enemy to destroy them. Instead, from out the awesome majesty of the cloud he spoke the glorious words of 20:2: "I am the LORD your God." Those words denote the imposition of a *relationship* between God and Israel, they describe God's *identity* as Israel's God and they as his people, they communicate God's *embrace* of idol-serving ex-slaves as his "treasured possession" (Ex 19:5). Here is privilege unsurpassed, majestic mercy and merciful majesty!

So Israel's respect for God of necessity must angle away from terror toward awe – and with the latter a sense of profound gratitude that expresses itself in willing obedience to the Ten Words of the Covenant God established between himself and this people (20:3-17; cf Dt 5:29; 6:2; 10:12f; 13:4). Clearly, grasping his majestic mercy means there is place only piety, trust, love, believing.[4]

The Origin of Fear

The question now arises as to the origin of these two contrasting responses to taking God seriously. The first use of the word "fear" (in Hebrew) in the Bible is in Gen 3:10, directly after humanity's rebellion against God in Paradise. Adam and Eve had previously come face to face with God in the Garden when they could enjoy his creative wisdom and his gracious care. They not only "clearly perceived" "his invisible attributes, namely, his eternal power and divine nature" (Rom 1:20) but their resulting respect for God angled distinctly in the direction of awe and adoration.

---

4   Cf Bavinck, *Reformed Dogmatics*, Vol 1, pg 237f: "This term [ie, *the fear of the Lord*] expresses the inner disposition of the devout Israelite toward the holy laws that the Lord has instructed him to keep.... This fear of the Lord passes into and is bound up with an assortment of other religious attitudes such as believing, trust, taking refuge in, leaning on, holding on to, hoping, expecting, even loving God. The Lord's claims do not remain outside of and above the Israelites as they object of their terror and fear but become the object of their love. They ponder them with their intellect and observe them with their will. They are their delight all day long. In the NT we encounter essentially the same view...."

That angling changed on the day they inexplicably transgressed his command. When the God whose majesty was displayed in every tree and flower called for them after their rebellion, Adam responded with saying, "I heard the sound of you in the garden, and I was afraid" (Hebrew: "fear"; Gen 3:10). Since the day of their creation, Adam and Eve knew that they had every reason to take God very seriously but now their sense of guilt on account of their high-handed rebellion filled them with terror before the God they had offended. Their *sin* meant that the presence of God had become a terrible thing. It was etched in their minds: this God is *too much God* for them to survive his righteous response to transgression; he is too overwhelming and they too puny to go toe to toe against him. He is the Creator, we the creature; he is the eternal God, we pinched off a piece of clay (Job 33:6) – yet we dared to defy him!

Fear, then, involves acknowledgment of two fundamental realities. The first is the awareness of the Lord's *God*ness, his infinite majesty, his almighty power, his righteous justice, etc. The second is the keen awareness of our humanity, our humble origins as dust-made-alive, our smallness and dependence on him – let alone the fact that we're sinners, arrogant rebels who ruined the creation he entrusted to our care. Taking this God seriously of necessity must awaken in the sinner a strong sense of terror in the face of his majesty. The only way this rightful terror can be replaced with some other emotion is when God himself enfolds the trembling sinner with his compassionate love – and then the terror of necessity must morph into trembling adoration.

Mercy's Cost

It needs to be understood that God's compassionate love does not come cheaply to him; the "seed of the woman" first mentioned in Gen 3:15 is ultimately his only eternal Son (John 1:1-3,14). It is the awareness of the divine price God would pay to rescue sinners from his own wrath that converts the sinner's terror into adoration (Rom 5:6ff).

Yet even this ultimate price fails to move the needle deeply enough into the territory of awe if the initial terror is shallow. A shrunken degree of terror, as if sin is no big thing or as if God is understanding or quick to overlook or too busy to notice my foibles, leads to a shrunken degree of awe. Conversely, a overpowering sense of God's righteous anger at my sins -even if (as we might say) we take just one piece of fruit from a forbidden tree- leads to deepest adoration for a God who put forward such a costly solution to my arrogant transgression.

The fear-known-as-terror, then, lies side by side with the fear-known-as-adoration; they are not polar opposites in depth or intensity. The bridge one travels from the one fear to the other is the cross of Jesus Christ. On the cross the horrid terror I deserve on account of my sin was poured onto God's own Son so that I might be forgiven of my sins and restored to God's family. Now the intensity of terror-filled fear may shift to an equally intense awe-filled fear of God.

Conversely, the worst response possible to this display of majestic mercy is that of "the wicked": "there is no fear of God before his eyes" (Ps 36:1). The absence of fear altogether, be it whether it angles in the direction of terror or in the direction of awe, speaks to a heart totally *unimpressed* by God's identity. It's arrogantly cancelling God, declaring him a nothing, his majesty non-existent, his mercy a non-event. It's truly the height of unbelief.

New Testament

We have thus far paid considerable attention to Old Testament material. Readers familiar with the Bible will know the apostle John's famous statement: "perfect love casts out fear" (1 John 4:18). The reader may in turn be tempted to conclude that the New Testament church ought not to devote much attention to the fear of God.

In reply we need first to insist that God has not changed over the generations or even the dispensations; recall his *simplicity*. People have not fundamentally changed either; we are still finite and remain rebels at heart (Rom 7:18). So the injunction repeated so often in Scripture to fear God, to respect him, to take him seriously, remains in force.

It is also gloriously true that God has displayed perfect love-for-sinners with his gracious gift of his only Son as our Savior (John

3:16). More, Christ Jesus has displayed ultimate love in his self-emptying sacrifice for sinners on the cross (John 13:1) as he bore the eternal wrath of God in our place. The blessed fruit of his work is that holy, almighty God has become our Father in Jesus Christ. So there is no longer place for the redeemed to be terrorized of God.

But perhaps most importantly, every New Testament believer needs to come to grips with the instruction of the apostle to the Hebrews. That apostle reminds us that we have not come to a *less impressive* place than Israel did at Mt Sinai but to a *more impressive* place. Mt Sinai was so terrifyingly awesome that Moses "trembled with fear" (Heb 12:21). But through the blessed work of Jesus Christ (cf Heb 9:26) the Hebrew Christians "have come to Mount Zion and to the city of the living God, the heavenly Jerusalem, and to innumerable angels in festal gathering, and to the assembly of the firstborn who are enrolled in heaven, and to God, the judge of all, and to the spirits of the righteous made perfect, and to Jesus, the mediator of a new covenant, and to the sprinkled blood that speaks a better word than the blood of Abel" (Heb 12:22-24). Might I say: Old Testament Israel came to Mt Sinai where God in turn was pleased to condescend in his majesty. God's New Testament people, by contrast, have come to God's own dwelling place in heaven. Talk about glorious progress for a people once exiled from God's Garden of Eden! So the apostle's command is fully predictable: "see that you do not refuse him who is speaking" (Heb 12:25). He explains: if Israel could not get away with refusing to heed God's words when God "warned them on earth", how much less will New Testament saints get away with refusing to heed when God "warns from heaven" (v. 25)! It leads to the pressing instruction that climaxes the apostle's line of thought: "let us offer God acceptable worship with reverence and awe, for our God is a consuming fire" (Heb 12:28f). Terrible as consuming fire is, the sort of fear that rightly typifies New Testament Christians angles distinctly in the direction of wonder and veneration.

I beg of my readers to have this point of revelation straight in our minds. The God of the New Testament dispensation is not a more relaxed, friendlier version of the sin-condemning God of the Old Testament. Rather, he is the same God as spoke to Adam and to Abraham, Isaac and Jacob, and revealed himself to Israel via Moses at Mt Sinai. The awful, hellish suffering unleashed upon Jesus Christ when the righteous wrath of this God upon our sins was poured on him illustrates the awe-full love and the awe-full hate of this God, his mercy and his justice, his infinite sovereignty and holiness and compassion. Jesus on Good Friday trembled with greater fear than Moses did at Mt Sinai when he pleaded with God to let this cup pass (Luke 22:42ff) and when he cried out his anguish that God had forsaken him (Mt 27:46). *Without* the mediating work of Jesus Christ, we sinners have no choice when we come face to face with God but to hide ourselves in any hole we can to escape his righteous wrath (see Rev 6:15ff). Conversely, *with* the mediating work of Jesus Christ, we sinners may confidently come into the presence of God (Heb 10:19) as adopted children. It is *Christ's* work that changes trembling fright to trembling awe – precisely as it was in the Old Testament dispensation.

Ethic

Such high appreciation for the abiding greatness of God makes unmistakably clear that there's no place for sloppiness in the service of this God. John Murray has said it well: "The fear of God is the soul of godliness." And later: "ethical integrity is grounded in and is the fruit of the fear of God".[5] Every mood I embrace, every thought I think, every word I speak, every action I undertake is done in the presence of this holy, glorious God who loathes rebellion so much that he vanquished his Son under the load of his infinite hatred of my sin. Awe, horror, amazement, fascination with God having done *that* to his Son instead of to guilty me can rightly lead to no other response than self-loathing in the face of my sins, horror that I've offended God so deeply, hatred of sin and determination to avoid sin, *terrified fear of God* as I see in the eye of my mind his face contorted with wrathful hate as his justice is poured out onto Jesus Christ – and then adoration, fascination, admiration, *God-praising fear* as I realize that I escape the penalty I deserve and instead get wrapped up for Jesus' sake into the arms of the God who adopted me into his divine family. "Praise the Lord, O my soul, and all that is within me, Praise his holy name!"

---

5   *Principles of Conduct*, pg 231f.

Postscript

Who we think God is has a most profound effect on our evaluation of ourselves. The smaller we think God is the smaller we conclude sin to be – and the more inflated we become in our own eyes. The gauge we need, then, to determine what we actually think about God is not our words or even our Confessions; the accurate gauge is our *conduct*. A high view of sin, with its accompanying aversion of sin, signals a high view of God; conversely, a low view of sin, with its accompanying relaxed attitude about sinning, betrays a low view of God. That is why David could say of people who had no issue with iniquity that "there is no fear of God before his eyes" (Ps 36:1).

I certainly would not want to say that Christians in today's western world have no fear of God before their eyes. But I'm afraid that many Christians in today's western world embrace a *shrunken* view of God – and the evidence lies in our conduct. I think of the nearly universal habit amongst western Christians to embrace love of stuff – as if happiness lies more in houses and marriage and freedom and holidays and vehicles and foods and family and job than in belonging to God and emptying self to live for him. I think of the tepid way in which we admonish each other in the face of sin as we dare not step on each other's toes lest we offend. I think of the way we have come to justify divorce and then let a divorcee utter a second oath to be faithful to a new spouse "till death us do part" while the first spouse is still living. I think of the way we condone withdrawal from the church or failure to meet with the saints or even to submit ourselves to the preaching of the gospel while Scripture tells us plainly that the church needs us and we need the church (eg, 1 Cor 12). I think of the casual dress code that typifies so much western church-going and the informal and colloquial manner in which we speak to God in prayer. Those *activities* are so far removed from the "reverence and awe" the inspired apostle enjoined his readers and they're reflective of what we really think of our God.

All in all, we're not so small in our own eyes anymore, we're not so dependent on almighty God for our needs, we're not so tainted with sin and prone to evil. Our self *in*flation has *de*valued God in our estimation. This needs repentance. And repentance requires humility, first to acknowledge that we're but dust, then to acknowledge that sovereign God created us from dust, then too to confess that we arrogantly rebelled against him and finally to grant -with holy fear- that God himself has become one of us in the person of his Son to redeem us from the horrid penalty we deserve. Humble and small thoughts of ourselves reflect exalted and glorious thoughts of God – be it fear-filled terror in the face of his righteous judgment or fear-filled adoration in the face of his gracious mercy in Jesus Christ.

Either way: *I'm small before him* and *he is great!* His love, his simplicity, his holiness, his sovereignty are so infinitely beyond me -pinched as I am off a piece of clay- that my posture before him can rightly be none other than reverential fear. That fear looks like eager obedience as I seek, across the board of life, to serve a God of such *God*ness.

www.ingramcontent.com/pod-product-compliance
Lightning Source LLC
Chambersburg PA
CBHW052205070526
44585CB00017B/2075